For Susan
Many c'n
this book.

MYSTIC MOUNTAIN
The Ascent to Love

By

John R. Sack

CyberScribe Publications

Copyright © 2013 John R. Sack. All rights reserved.

No part of this book may be reproduced or transmitted in any form or by any means, electronic or mechanical, including photocopying, recording or by any information storage and retrieval system without permission in writing from the author. Address inquiries to:

CyberScribe Publications
9700 Sterling Creek Road
Jacksonville, OR 97530
Email: cyberscribe2@hotmail.com

ISBN 978-1-49-237556-2

Oh the mind, mind has mountains, cliffs of fall,
Frightful, sheer, no-man-fathomed.
Hold them cheap who ne'er hung there.
—Gerard Manley Hopkins

Well, people sees you far up the line
and they don't see all the hills you come over
and all the mountains you clumb to get there.
—Mahalia Jackson

Who shall climb the mountain of the Lord?
Who shall stand in his holy place?
Those with clean hands and pure heart,
Who desire not worthless things.
—Psalm 24

Contents

Introduction: Of Ages and Stages 6
    Stages of Awakening 6
    Markers on the Spiritual Way 13

Chapter 1. In the Beginning 17
    The Call 18
    Sloughing Off the Dead Skin 25
    Practice, Practice, Practice 29
        The high road 31
        Verbal prayer 33
        Spiritual reading 35
        Meditation, reflection and recollection 38
        Solitude and silence 40
        Self-knowledge 42
        Dealing with dualism 49
    Formal Religion and the Mystic Way 53

Chapter 2. The Positive Way 61
    Seeking God's Face 61
    The Near and Far God 67
    God and I are One 70
        Heirs of God through adoption 75
        Some side-effects of breakthrough 77
    After the Breakthrough 80
        Service 85
        A deeper surrender 88
        Understanding suffering 92
    Cosmic Prayer and Beginning Contemplation 98
        The universal priesthood 98
        From meditation to contemplation 99
        Infused prayer 101
        Spiritual sleep 104

Chapter 3. The High Desert 107

> The Negative Way 108
> Rebirth in Spirit and Fire 110
> > *Another name for Spirit 113*
> > *Surrendering to Love 115*
>
> Into the Dark 117
> > *Dark contemplation 119*
> > *Ecstasy and rapture 122*
> > *The death of ego 124*
> > *The abyss of poverty 129*
> > *Blessed are the poor in spirit 131*
> > *The dark nights 135*
> > *Suffering in darkness 136*

Chapter 4. Falling in Love with Love 143

> The Transformed Body and Personality 146
> The Convergence of the Twain 152
> After Enlightenment: The Return 156
> > *Loving the dear neighbor 158*
> > *The evolving cosmic plan 162*
> > *Contemplation vs. action 164*
> > *The bodhisattva 168*

Chapter 5. Death, the Ultimate Breakthrough 171

> Eterne and Return 171
> > *The Ascent through awareness and love 172*
> > *Strangers in a strange land 174*
>
> Approaching Death 176
> Fear of Dying 177
> Why, I? 180
> Life after Death 183

Suggested Reading 189

Introduction: Of Ages and Stages

This is a tale of the human journey, the pilgrimage that begins in the nakedness of birth and occupies all the days and nights of our lives. Had we circled earth at the turn of the last century, we had, on average, 31 years to complete the course. By the year 2000, worldwide life expectancy had risen to 67. In the United States where I am writing, eight decades is no longer an exceptional age and the number of centenarians increased from 32,194 in 1980 to 71,944 in 2010. Ours is the longest-lived generation in recorded history and, while it's true that longevity can be a mixed blessing, the elder explosion does harbor the potential for unparalleled soul work. Our maturing cultures have been invited to a previously inconceivable growth in wisdom—in the words of Joseph Campbell, *such wisdom as belongs rather to experienced old age than to poetically fantasizing youth*, wisdom for our elder years.

Stages of Awakening

Our story erupts in the density of flesh but later mutates into a tale of the spirit and its meandering path back to Origin. Our first act is a howl of protest as we are pulled from the soothing darkness of the womb. At this point, according to Jewish tradition, we know everything, but then the angel Leila (Laylah) touches our lips, creating the crease beneath our nose, and all is forgotten. We enter the glare of daylight in square one. As yet, we make no distinction between our universe and us. If we are cold, the world is cold; if we are hungry, the whole world hungers.

Our preparation for life on planet earth begins shortly afterward as we slowly emerge from the unity of *beginner's mind* into the diversity of form. We come to view the face above the cradle as separate from us. The smiling adoration of that face suggests we are also the center of whatever plane we've entered. We continue to live in the *now* at that instant, but soon learn to add the separation of time—past, present and future. "When you were little, your favorite food was yoghurt. ... You can play outdoors until dinner. ... Next year you can start preschool."

As our sense of identity develops, we accept that we are distinct from our fellows and, in fact, are separate from *everything* else in our knowable world—that cow, that whiff of incense, that cloud, that song—everything. We may even reach our productive years believing our bodies are isolated from the products of our minds. By then, we likely will have buried every aspect of ourselves that embarrassed us early on or that we have been told is *wrong* or is frowned upon in our particular culture. Practically speaking, we emerge from the undifferentiating oneness of the newborn into the multiplicity and self-centeredness that are exactly the set of tools we need to survive on earth. We recognize ourselves as unique bodies and minds, members of a race or interracial tribe, a nation and society, with an accumulation of thoughts and beliefs and a skill set. We're ready to take on the world!

In our early, neophyte decades we typically are students, unmarried workers or married householders, struggling to afford food, shelter and utilities, preoccupied with exams or job reviews, paying down school loans, auto loans, charge cards and mortgages, overtaxed, raising children, working on relations, picking up the pieces when they fail. The emphasis is on success, comfort and accumulation—achieving, buying and owning while perhaps stockpiling weapons to guard what we've acquired. Our marching orders are clear: finish school, get a good job, buy a house, car(s), big TV and powerful computer, marry and pass on our genes and values to the kids—all of that which Zorba the Greek summarized as *the whole catastrophe.*

Perhaps we even achieve the Confucian ideal of *good people*—compassionate towards others, tolerant of their beliefs, using knowledge and power wisely. For many, such attainment is *good enough* and as far as we care to hike up the trail of virtue. And why shouldn't it be? We learn from childhood in our schools and through our political and religious institutions that this ideal of the moral person, the good citizen, is the epitome of worthy behavior. We may sleep at night with an easy conscience without having had one transcendent thought during the day.

Skimming through life has its downside, however. We may find ourselves in our comfortable homes, not in the grip of some dark force, but instead suspended in triviality, entangled in our security blankets, staunchly defending images of ourselves built up over decades, numb to the *further* invitation that whispers below the surface of mere existence—nothing less than a divine beckoning to unfamiliar depths. We won't have read anything in our schoolbooks about the mysterious Spirit hiding at our core, however, for our studies penetrate at most to the level of the psyche and even that level of awareness is often reduced to brain mechanics. What we call *depth psychology* is a misnomer for it doesn't penetrate to the deepest part of us, to the innermost core of our spirit where the Godhead dwells.

While we may feel secure inside our pleasure domes, ultimately we can't be fulfilled. We can mount the ladder of success, accumulating prizes on each rung, only to discover at the top that it leans against a Hollywood façade. There's nothing there but more stuff. Nevertheless, we usually opt for safety and cling to this sham set rather than descend through darkness the reverse ladder of humility, the one that offers unfathomable Love in the deepest reaches of an indiscernible abyss.

We can't handle mystery. Most of us are more comfortable with the activities of *subsistence* than the notion of free-floating in an enigma of pure *being*. We fear in particular the riddle of our own interiors, and so we cleave to the external. Annie Dillard deplored such thinking! *We should amass half-dressed in long lines like tribesmen*, she wrote, *shake gourds at each other to wake up. Instead, we watch television and miss the show.*

A Hasidic tale of Rabbi Barukh of Mezbizh tells how his grandson Yehiel was playing hide-and-seek with another boy. He hid himself well and waited for his playmate to find him, but the boy never came. Finally Yehiel came out of his hiding place, but the other boy was gone, and he realized that his friend hadn't even bothered to look for him. Disconsolate, he ran to his grandfather in tears. The Rabbi too began to weep and told his grandson, "God says the same thing: *I hide, but no one wants to seek me.*"

When we *do* back down the ladder, it is because we feel an inexplicable urge to slough off this seemingly pointless and hamstrung existence with its deadening concessions—shed it like a snake ridding itself of tattered, useless skin. Surely there has to be further purpose to our years here beyond the fascinations that captivate us and our peers. We're not merely naked apes responding to territorial imperatives, are we? And what was that subtle stirring, that brief longing that sparked within us in midlife, leaving us bewildered, yet wanting more? From such unrest the search for that hidden *something beyond* begins.

In the midst of such wondering, we may be further intrigued by a cloud-shrouded pinnacle visible in the distance. "Oh, you mean Mystic Mountain," a voice replies to our question. *And what is Mystic Mountain*, we ask? We've heard of the *mystic way*, and felt a certain curiosity about its meaning. But the word *mystic* can confuse us also, particularly if we've grown up in the West. We may have heard from our religious institutions, even those with strong traditions of mysticism, that this form of spirituality is risky, a possible snare of the dark side, or that we may sink forever into the quicksand of psychosis.

> Mystical teachings are enticing, powerful, and potentially dangerous. The spiritual seeker soon discovers that he or she is not exploring something *up there*, but rather the *beyond* that lies within. Letting go of traditional notions of God and self can be both liberating and terrifying. In the words of Isaac of Akko: *Strive to see supernal light, for I have brought you into a vast ocean. Be careful! Strive to see, yet escape drowning.*[1]

And yet ... and yet ... the lure continues to dance before us. Now is when the more inquisitive and courageous among us find ourselves wanting to probe more deeply the beliefs spoon-fed us in youth. We want answers to the large questions of life that resonate on the same frequency as our intuition. Intuition,

---

[1] Daniel C. Matt, *The Essential Kabbalah*, (New York: HarperCollins, 1995), p. 17

in turn, urges us to step within, to take a first, cautious peek around the *terra incognita* that is our interior landscape.

This movement might be gradual and natural, a gentle slide from our previous life in the general direction of the new. Just as likely, however, change will be imposed upon us by a traumatic event, a serious illness or accident, hitting bottom emotionally or materially, the death of a loved one, the disruption of war or other such painful event screaming at us: *Pay attention! In a heartbeat you can lose all this you thought was important.*

None of this is meant to denigrate the significance of our youthful years. These early attempts at flight, the vapor trails that illumine our pasts are, in fact, the necessary prelude of our wisdom years, the liftoff from which mature spirituality can soar. Even while we strive to survive and advance through the early stages of normal human development, we constantly encounter lessons and gifts that point beyond. These may include faint glimmerings of a distant and incomprehensible Love beyond measure!

Each step forward offers its own invaluable contribution to the long-term health of our body, mind, psyche and spirit. Sentient life itself is the first such gift, for only in this form can we even aspire to know and participate in divine Love. As Buddha Shakyamuni put it, *it is not easy to be reborn as a human being. It is rarer than for a one-eyed turtle, who rises to the surface only once every hundred years, to push his neck through a wooden yoke with one hole that floats on the surface of the wide ocean.* We can attribute his comparison to poetic license given the seven billion of us sharing the planet, but his image speaks clearly to the precious value of existence and the need to put our priceless years, this flash of life, to good use.

> Of all the created things or beings of the universe, it is the two-legged men alone who, if they purify and humble themselves, may become one with—or may know—*Wakan-Taka.*
>
> —Black Elk

We experience numerous hints of something infinite as we develop. For example, we feel oneness with a loving other in our mother's womb and drink in affection at her breast. When our father takes our hand as we cross the street, he prefigures the hand reaching out across eternity. We often have our first experience of the divine as children, before we enter into the busy-ness of life.

As a six-year-old, I lounged high in the branches of an oak tree, asking the tree about its own beginning and sapling years. I knew enough about plant propagation to realize it had grown from an acorn that had fallen from an older oak and reasoned backwards to the original tree or seed and its source in creation—that is to Thomas Aquinas' first proof for the existence of God. (I, like Thomas, knew nothing of evolution.) My wife had a similar childhood connection while gazing into the golden throat of a wild lily. Baby contemplatives we were, innately connected with the sacred, until that original brilliance faded in the dull light of everyday. I suspect most people reading this book have similar memories.

In elementary school we learn to play and cooperate with other children and to connect with all creation through nature, marveling at the Milky Way or a colony of ants. It's no wonder that my most cherished "toy" as a child was a microscope. We begin to think independently as teens, rehearsing the obligatory withdrawal from our parents and to rebel against the blind acceptance of authority. We practice perseverance as students, then caring and responsibility towards our families and neighbors as householders.

Many of the current generation of elders practiced a form of mysticism while relatively young, in the 1960s and 1970s, when we were drawn eastward to satisfy some interior itch. There we learned Buddhist and Hindu methods of meditation and contemplation. We sat in caves or temples in the lotus position while the kundalini energy shook our spines and left us so still we nearly forgot to breath. Gurus taught us how to use mantras as we prayed, phrases such as the *so-ham* japa, "I am That" or *tat tvam asi*, "You are It" that embodied the preposterous notion: *I and the Divine are One*. What a concept! Along with incredible papaya, we had a taste of Self as Pure Being. Had we proposed this aloud in North America a century ago, we might have ended in an asylum. In medieval Europe, the Inquisition would have called us kindling.

And so the journey resumes as we approach our wisdom years. That voice from within beckons and we turn inward, trying to plumb its source. We can respect and incorporate what we learned as youth, but a profound dissatisfaction tells us that it's time to move beyond that mindset. We've come to understand that the ego we've created and its playthings cannot birth the spirituality we need to become whole people, that what we truly desire and what our surroundings have to offer are widely different. We strongly suspect that the being we *thought* we were is but a *poseur* clothed in gaudy masquerade.

Increased interiority carries within it an equal indifference to the external. We become sated with consumerism and the cacophony of media-driven babble. Former values and activities no longer satisfy and lose their sense of urgency. We can now recognize their lack of staying power, their lack of substance. The exterior world assumes an aura of strangeness and we set foot into a landscape as different from what we've known as the muggle- versus wizard-worlds in the Harry Potter series.

Interior focus, then, and not necessarily seniority, is the common denominator among the growing number of sages among us. In India, the final two of the four stages of life are the *Vanaprasta* (semi-retired hermit), and the *Sannyasi* (wandering ascetic), periods of service and renunciation. But although the idleness afforded by retirement helps—providing time to read and ruminate, to serve and to pray—some turn within early in life. Others of our species, sad to say, never "get it" and approach death in a state of bitterness, as the last in a series of rancid pills life has forced them to swallow. Grace, or Spirit, flows when and where it will, and those to whom it flows sooner, rather than later, can only prostrate themselves in thanks and gratitude.

The research of developmental and transpersonal psychologists would suggest that less than 2% of us presently accept the invitation to transcend the superficial life, althoughtheir studies also suggest the potential for many more wise elders as the boomers age.² We can communicate globally now also, allowing us to link to others walking the way. We may find to our surprise and possible bewilderment that we are on the cutting edge of human evolution.

Markers on the Spiritual Way

Once we take the first step inward, we discover that the spiritual quest is a pilgrim's progress. God's cosmos is *endlessly becoming*, the sense in which the name *God* is a verb, and each of us is a small part of that evolution. The path home to our source and pure *being* is a journey of unending discovery and our spiritual growth, as a consequence, will be equally ongoing until our deaths (if not beyond).

We join a host of brother and sister pilgrims, each at different mileposts on the route. Given our human tendency to categorize, each wisdom tradition has attached its metaphors to the major landmarks of the journey. Whether we practice the Buddhist eight-fold way, climb the cosmic tree of the sefirot to Keter (or No-thing-ness), wander through the seven dwellings of Teresa of Avila's *Interior Castle*, or follow the trails broken by Lao Tzu, Ibn Al-Ghazali or Ādi Śaṅkara, is largely determined by our temperaments and the culture into which we were born. The language and symbols used to describe the indescribable likewise depend largely on the background of the mystic trying to portray them. All paths ultimately are sacred for they share an impulse towards the Absolute.

The way described in these pages, then, is that which most reflects my own experience, study and imagination, although I obviously hope readers will find it personally relevant as well. Clearly, the answers I've found in my heart cannot correspond exactly to the longing in yours. Look on this effort, then, as one man's take on the mystic way, one among numerous guides describing variations of the journey. Hopefully it will point you to other helpful resources and also be a work to which you can return frequently over the years as your pilgrimage evolves.

---

² See, for example, Don Beck and Chris Cowan, *Spiral Dynamics: Mastering Values, Leadership and Change*, (Cambridge, MA: Blackwell Publishers, 1995).

With that disclaimer, my favored vision of the spiritual dance is a three-step, one that parallels the three steps of enlightenment that support the *Throne of Isis* in the ancient mystery schools:

- the *active* phase of purgation, our response to Love's call, when with the aid and encouragement of Grace, we do all in our power to reorient our lives towards the infinite;
- the transition from the *active* phase to *passivity*, a period of respite and illumination;
- the *passive* phase of mastery as we approach perfection, when there is little we can do except show up each day and make ourselves available to the inpouring of Grace. Progress comes at God's pace, subject to God's will.

We're not totally passive in this third phase, however. Our job remains to *prepare* ourselves to receive the influx of Love—even as we try to stay out of its way. We continue our attempts to empty ourselves of all that does not point us toward God or that still stands as an obstacle between us and shared, Ultimate Being.

To the active-passive three-step I would add a pirouette spun specifically by those who reach the apex of the third movement:

- a return to active life, when fully enlightened, human-divine beings retrace their steps down the mountain as the servants of all, when compassion trumps contemplation and we discover to our surprise that Martha, not Mary, chose the better part.

The least bit of experience of this journey quickly shows us that these phases overlap. "Previews of coming attractions" also break into our early efforts, giving us a glimpse of higher levels of consciousness and whetting our appetite for those levels. They are meant to encourage us.

Artificial separations between these steps offer murky lines of demarcation at best. But what else can we expect when we set out on a largely uncharted way that differs for each traveler, a way that cannot be mapped because in truth it is no way, a non-way that meanders in obscurity along a path that can disappear at any moment, that leaves us wavering between doubt and trust, and finally requires of us a gigantic leap into an abyss of nothingness?

One particularly pointless exercise is wondering where we stand in this journey at any given moment. Psychotherapist James Finley tells the story of a meeting he had with Thomas Merton, his spiritual director during his young period in a Trappist monastery. He had been reading Teresa's *Interior Castle* and suggested that he felt he'd entered the fourth mansion, the transition between the active and passive ways, but if Father Merton thought he was still in the third, he could accept that. Merton's response: *It's none of your damn business which mansion you're in.* And that is true. Over and over, we impatient seekers must remind ourselves that grace and transformation flow at God's pace, according to God's will, and in ways that may often seem capricious or unsettling to our miniscule minds.

A favorite metaphor of spiritual authors compares the soul to a droplet submerged in a limitless ocean of Light. Expanding this image, we might suggest that during the most visible decades of our lives, we rise on the crest of a wave, displaying to all our fellow beings the brilliance of our ego, the sparkling froth we've created. But later, during our wisdom years, we succumb to the ocean's pull and allow ourselves to spill peacefully once more into the sea of our origin.

> Enlightenment for a wave
> is the moment it realizes it is water.
> At that moment, all fear of death disappears.
> —Thich Nhat Hanh

Once distinctions fuse into unity, once we merge with the sea, we can review the flow of our lives and realize that we have in truth traveled but *one* way, and this one, sometimes baffling way includes all the survival tactics of our youth. Between the profound silence that precedes our birth into humanity and the source of mystery that awaits us at death, the secular and the sacred, the physical and the spiritual, are fundamentally joined. But this is a discovery that lies well beyond the trailhead.

We set out on our way, then, with whatever awareness we possess at this moment, from whatever place we find ourselves presently positioned. It's time to awaken, or reawaken, to mystery and to trace it to its origin!

> Look, Master, at this realm of flowers and happy creatures—of phoenixes, cranes and deer. Is it not a better place indeed than the haunted deserts through which you and I have passed? Tripitaka murmured his thanks, and with a strange feeling of lightness and exhilaration, they all set off up the Holy Mountain.
>
> —Wu Ch'êng-ên, *Monkey*

Chapter 1. In the Beginning

A Celtic proverb says that heaven and earth are only three feet apart. Actually, they are much nearer than that. They interweave in a fantastic temporal-timeless tapestry that lets us pass between them with increasing ease as our spirituality deepens.

Initially our feet are firmly mired on this planet. Threshold creatures, when we do approach deity, we use the limited notions and names we learned as children: God, Goddess, Trinity, Word, Truth, Light, Allah, Yahweh, El or Elohim, Atman, Osiris, Great Spirit, Jesus, Krishna, Ra and Tao. In the early part of this work, I use these traditional labels when referring to Divinity as imagined by humans through images, attributes, or gender—the God or Goddess who cradles us in "his hands" or "her arms"—the God we created in our likeness to repay "him" for creating us in "his" likeness. Because we are trying to name the Nameless, however, even attempts to see beyond the imagery, using terms like Ground of Being, Source, Infinite, Void, No-Thing-Ness, One, Ein Sof, Brahman, Ultimate Reality, or Supreme Being all fall short. The Spirit that can be named is only a human representation of unnamable, ineffable, pure existence.

Still we must use some sound in our attempts to express the inexpressible. Anselm of Canterbury defined God as the unknowable and rather cumbersome *something-than-which-nothing-greater-can-be-thought*. As our journey progresses, I'll generally use Augustine's shorter term, *That-Which-Is* or *Godhead* or simply *That* or *It*, to refer to the essence that has ever been—totally *beyond* imagination, the "Is-Ness" of Being if you will. No word, image or symbol rooted in earthly experience can capture Its essence—*neti, neti*, not this, not this—but we do the best we can with the language we have, and absolute Being, "I AM," seems to be the closest our limited language can come to speaking the unutterable. In truth, we might summarize the mystic way as a movement from the *I, me, my* and *mine* of the small egoic self to that pure and essential *I AM* (or simply *AM*), the true Self, a movement that begins with an invitation from within.

The Call

For some the call comes as gently as a beautiful sight or sound that activates a long-neglected yearning. Some it strikes forcefully, like a slap from a Zen master, demanding their attention so they can hear in the ensuing stillness: *Return to me, with all your heart ... long have I waited for your coming.*

Long have I waited for your coming! How sweet is that!

Teresa of Avila compared it to a shepherd whistling to his flock, so softly that his sheep can barely hear him. Augustine heard it while walking in his garden. Petru Dumitriu paused halfway down his staircase to remove his glasses and was inexplicably overwhelmed with gratitude towards the Being whose existence he'd doubted until that moment. Paul of Tarsus, on the other hand, was by his own account violently knocked to the ground, personally chewed out by Jesus, and temporarily blinded.

The call is the energizer of the spiritual search. It often begins with a period of disquiet, a questioning. "What is life really about?" or as a poet might put it more succinctly, "Why I? And just who is this *I* being called to set out on a spiritual quest?" Even more importantly, "Who is it that I'm pursuing, or conversely, who is *the hound of heaven* dogging me?" These questions are fundamental to the spiritual quest because they lead us from self-centered, ego-centric focus on our small selves, to a *theocentric* life focused on God.

It might appear that the teachings of the Christ or the Buddha—rejecting power, wealth, violence and war in favor of enlightening the world through the power of love—can only be lived outside modern social structures. We can retire to a monastery or cave *OR* we can shed our former mentality even as we remain within a nonreligious setting, living in the world but not being part of it.

That's the most astounding aspect of the call. It can come to *anyone*, not just to the famous "saints." Each of us on the planet, regardless of cultural background and no matter how badly we've messed up the first segment of our lives, whether we be prophets or pariahs, are eligible for "sainthood." Even the official saints began their quest for God as people much like us. Obviously, not all of us can end as majestic redwoods in the celestial arboretum, but even the ferns and flowers and leathery-leafed salal, the tiniest ivy groundcover, are lovely and beloved.

I can guarantee up front that the call will be as persistent as convent bells beckoning nuns to chapel. It is irresistible and as it intensifies, it will prompt a genuine redirection of our lives. Like iron filings scattered across a vast table, we are tugged inexorably towards God, the all-powerful magnet. We are likely to encounter bumps, drag created by the rough grain of the surface, or obstacles on the tabletop that can shunt us onto detours, but the call is nonetheless insistent. If someone were to ask at this point why we want to set out on such an unfathomable way, we could only throw up our hands and answer, "Because I must"—the same reason sculptors chisel or birds fly.

To set out on the mystic way is to open ourselves to the eternal in the day-to-day here and now to whatever extent we are presently capable. Responding to the call, we waken to a startling, embryonic awareness, one that immediately sets up in opposition to the often silly world of illusion in which we've lived until now. When this wakening pierces all the way through to our hearts, we feel encouraged to take the first step in the proverbial journey of a thousand miles.

We set out across our inner landscapes like the travelers in Sesshu's long scroll, following winding paths through ever-changing terrain, initially dwarfed by the forests and cliffs that soar above us, in search of a monastery or inn to rest along the way. We still encounter raucous crowds in the busy marketplace, at times relax in the silence of an isolated village where sampans bob in a sheltered cove, and always long to escape into the distance where our glorious, higher Self awaits. As we progress, the markets become more rare, the quiet villages more common, and the wish to reach our destination more intense. We climb secluded trails spiraling up and around the holy mountain, at times slowed by switchbacks on the steeper ascents. Above the tree line we wander through both pleasant meadows and arid deserts and higher still through clouds towards our unseen goal. All the while we shed masks and costumes, thoughts, beliefs and emotions, our small selves and their agendas until, breaking through the clouds into the brilliant sunshine at the summit, we find ourselves prostrate and naked before the naked Beloved.

In the tradition of Asian art, this ascent to Love is measured by the changing of the seasons, and we sense already that, in the end, it will exhaust all the seasons left to us. A journey of such magnitude cannot be rushed, however. It deserves all the time we can devote to it and, in fact, will require that our devotion be total. We also hope that each round of seasons will find us in a better, higher and more joyful place, with a more spacious vista, than the year before.

The tracks we follow in this ascent are as diverse as the cultures and spiritual traditions into which we were born, as unique as the personas we created in our earliest decades. Love draws us along countless routes. Divinity blazes out at us from every aspect of creation and in reality, we do not choose our spiritual path; the path chooses us. Consequently, it's very clear that we have no basis for telling others they're on the wrong path, or that ours is the only right way. Right for us, but perhaps disastrous for another seeker.

This is a good time to assess our current attempts at spirituality. If the religion or culture in which we were raised is not growing us, now is our opportunity to find a way that will. Don't be afraid to explore other wisdom traditions during this initial period. All contain a shard of, though none have a monopoly on, Truth. The more shards you can gather, the closer you'll come to reassembling the entire vessel that shattered, according to legend, when it once-upon-a-time fell from heaven to earth.

> In the Garden of the Brotherhood, each shall follow his own path, and each shall commune with his own heart, for in the infinite Garden there are many and diverse flowers.
>
> —Jesus, *The Essene Gospel of Peace*

The call is generally seen as the critical moment of *conversion*, or *turning back*, in the spiritual journey. Those of us asked to walk this road are without exception prodigals desperate to return to our Father's house, the Divine within us, *nearer to us than we are to ourselves* to paraphrase Augustine. And like the father in the story of the prodigal son, God sees us coming from afar and rushes to meet us on the way. The path to which we are setting foot can also be entered from the far end and be assured that God will meet us halfway.

Divinity calls out to each of us as It once appealed to the Israelites in Hosea, couching Its words in warmth and even the promise of union between our human spirit and the Beloved: *I am going to lure her and lead her out into the wilderness and speak to her heart. ... I will betroth you to myself forever, betroth you with integrity and justice, and tenderness and love; I will betroth you to myself with faithfulness, and you will come to know Yahweh* (Hosea, 2:16, 21-22). The hunger for union, whether or not it is fully understood, is what sets our spirits in motion and perhaps—in the midst of one dark night—*on fire*.

However we envision the mystic way, understand from the outset that it *is* a pilgrimage, meaning it will *insist* that we change and that it includes no free passes or shortcuts. We are very much works in progress. We have a lifetime of effort ahead of us and will undergo endless breakthroughs and transformation in the process, nothing less than a reenactment of the archetypal hero's journey:

> Where we had thought to find an abomination, we shall find a god; where we had thought to slay another, we shall slay ourselves; where we had thought to travel outwards, we shall come to the center of our own existence; where we had thought to be alone, we shall be with all the world.[3]

A certain irony hides within the heart of this way that eventually will become clear to us. To see this irony, however, we need a level of awareness not granted at the outset. Our first step in search of the Divine, you see, is actually a step *away*, as Divinity, even before the beginning, has dwelt within us, as us. We cannot see That we seek because It, and not us, is doing the looking. We are far short of the vantage Meister Eckhart reached when he exclaimed: *the eye through which I see God is the same eye through which God sees me!*

---

[3] Joseph Campbell, *The Hero With a Thousand Faces*, (Novato: New World Library, 3rd Edition, 2008)

Lao Tzu wrote, *the further you go, the less you know. Thus the sage knows without traveling.* The Sufi mystic and poet Rûmî likewise sang to his Beloved:

> I assumed you were outside me,
> but now that you've dropped the veil,
> I realize you are the One
> I left behind with my first step.

Rûmî's words call to mind Colonel Percy Fawcett, a British surveyor and explorer (and inspiration for the Indiana Jones movies) who disappeared in the Mato Grosso region of the Amazon in 1925. He sought a lost civilization that he called the City of Z. He felt he'd failed in his quest, but the findings of a later archeologist, Michael Heckenberger, and views from Google Earth suggest he might have been standing in the very heart of the city when he was killed by hostile tribesmen. He didn't recognize what he'd discovered because he was expecting European-style ruins with stone walls and foundations, but Heckenberger found instead the decomposed remains of wood and palm buildings, moats, dirt roads, earthen mounds and wooden stockades. There's not a lot of rock in the Amazon. The point here for us is that, like Fawcett, we *already are* where we hope to be. It's already done. We don't recognize our good fortune, however, partly because of our preconceived notions of the Godhead and what the ego says oneness with the Divine should be like. We're looking for what isn't, and was never, there.

Clearly we need to awaken our awareness to another, far more expansive understanding. This need is another way to describe the desperate longing that impels us—the search for the missing piece, the hope that one day God *will* lead us through the tangled jungle concealing the secret sanctuary in the deepest recess of our being. Because the tangle remains, however, because the small self keeps us snagged in *samsara*, because our ego-driven minds want to direct the adventure, we feel we need to set out in search of this place where we hope to find both God and ourselves. Geoffrey Chaucer described this wanderlust in the Prologue to his *Canterbury Tales*:

> Thanne longen folk to goon on pilgrimages,
> And palmeres for to seken straunge strondes
> To ferne halwes, kowthe in sondry londes.

God is at home, but we are abroad Meister Eckhart lamented, echoing Augustine's *You were within, but I was without.* We entertain a zillion beliefs about God, about ourselves and about our inner and outer worlds, while the simple Truth, the wholeness of all being, of all becoming, eludes us. We are not unlike shamans on "soul retrieval" journeys, trying to gather up bits of shattered "soul" here and there, but we miss the larger realization that the "here and there" are encompassed in a single frame.

The greatest source of uneasiness in this life is the failure to see our oneness with Divinity, the destructive assumption that *we are separate from That-Which-Is*. The mystic way, the road home, is but a metaphor for our attempts, aided by Love, to regain this primal awareness. We knew such unity before we took form; the distortions we created or that were foisted upon us in our young years, however, convinced us that we exist apart from God. These fabrications are the mud we must hose away before we can appreciate the brilliance of the precious gem. What we need to do (or undo) on the mystic way therefore becomes obvious! We must find, bring to light and then *become* That which, paradoxically, we have always been. And so, pilgrims and palmers, the spiritually halt and lame, we set out one dim predawn in the direction of Mystic Mountain, which we hope will be the mount of our transfiguration. Why can it not be today, this next moment?

Assured that we will have divine help along the way, we can share Paul's conviction that our strength is in our weakness. Confronting and embracing our imperfection from the outset, we are freed to receive divine compassion, the true source of healing. Moreover, because the God who formed us and loves us is asking for our love in return, we can be sure we were sent into this world with at least a latent capacity to unleash such love. We may even guess (correctly) that loving God is our natural state.

While we cannot see it at first, divine Love, when the time is right, will well up within us to burn away our self-infatuation in Its crucible of purgation. A moment will come when we will see reality just as it is, from the place where we stand, in a state of *utter emptiness*. Meanwhile, our human nature compels us to *do something*, and so we respond to God's invitation by taking action, instigating a lengthy period of preparation.

Instinct, another word for inner guidance, informs us that to reach the heights of Mystic Mountain we must start by lightening our packs. We also will need to rejuvenate those physical, mental and spiritual aspects of ourselves that remain after we have unburdened, strengthening them like young muscles, preparing for the steep climb ahead. This is not the yellow-brick road we're planning to hike, nor the level plains of Kansas.

We could compare our starting situation to an average runner being coached and conditioned for a marathon. The trainee would not only strengthen the legs and lower body, but also the arms and shoulders that provide extra drive, build a base of endurance by jogging long, steady miles, alternate fast and slow segments (fartleks) during these runs, and begin shorter sprints to build speed and stamina. Added to these road and track workouts would be concerns about diet, adequate sleep, cross-training, footwear and other running gear. Distance conditioning quickly would become an all-consuming way of life. Dedicated runners are totally absorbed in their passion, and this likewise is the only option for the soul devoted to the mystic way. We're in for a marathon, or more precisely, an ultramarathon.

Self-stripping and detachment therefore define the first steps of our pilgrimage, starting at the overgrown base of the mountain. And what a snarled mess it is! We'll need machetes to hack a path through this tangle! Because we are clearing the accumulation of a lifetime, we also can expect to meet fierce resistance from the deeply-rooted ego.

> The places where we are stuck, those difficult layers of fear and attachment, the points of self-delusion and unworthiness we will encounter are many. They come in everyone's practice, and the more educated and competent

we believe ourselves to be, the slower the climb and the more foolhardy our falls.
—Jack Kornfield

The course will be uneven and inconsistent for us novice mystics. We may find ourselves one day in a glade luxuriating in the warmth of a sunny afternoon, the next day bogged down in a quagmire of depression, and the following day totally ensnared in the thickets of our pasts. We may find ourselves despairing with Dante,

> In the middle of the journey of my life
> I found myself inside a dark wood,
> for I had lost the straight path.
> Oh, how hard a thing it is to tell
> of that savage forest, harsh and dense ...
> So bitter—death is hardly more severe.
> —Dante, *Inferno*, Canto 1, 1-7

Our aspiration from the outset is that we may one day become That we seek, that given time enough and breakthroughs enough we may be united to the Beloved. The offering we wish to lay before the Godhead at that moment is the total transformation of our small selves, to return our spirits to the Beloved in the condition we originally received them.

If it's any consolation as we start out, the preparation phase of the journey—often over the course of years and decades—is the hardest part of the way, as well as a severe test of our commitment and perseverance. But with detachment and spiritual practice comes a sense of equilibrium we likely have never before experienced. We will no longer ride the emotional roller coaster connected to the negative (and positive) happenings that typically are part of everyday experience.

Sloughing Off the Dead Skin

Some years ago, my daughter and I traveled to Roncesvalles in the Pyrenees bordering France and Spain. Our goal was to hike as much of the Camino de Santiago pilgrims' route across northern Spain as we could manage during her 3-week work vacation. Veterans of the Camino eyed my backpack and predicted I would toss most of its content within a week. They could have said, *by tomorrow morning.*

So begins the trek up Mystic Mountain. The first thing we discover about this trip, advice that will echo repeatedly as we ascend the mountain, is that we must learn to let go. The nature and form of this surrender intensifies at higher levels, but self-denial and dissolution of our egos and all that clings to them are required at each stage.

If we are sincere in our pursuit of the way, we have no choice but to release our desires, attachments and addictions, our oh-so-carefully-crafted personas and versions of *reality*. We need to let go of anything that will weight us down. Much of this is not harmful or hurtful, to us or anyone else, but must be jettisoned simply because it doesn't align with our new priorities. To the converts of Corinth who said *for me nothing is forbidden*, Paul responded, *maybe, but not everything does good* (Corinthians 6:12). From here on, we need to focus solely on those things and activities that advance us spiritually.

This is not to say we'll empty our packs immediately. That we certainly will not! We have taken on a Herculean task, laboring to offload years of painstakingly created false identities. Addictions and compulsions in particular do not just disappear because we want them to. Releasing long-held beliefs can be gut-wrenching. But with patience, with perseverance, the ego's hold on us will weaken and the authentic Self will grow stronger. Mooji once observed that *the ego is the heaviest thing in the world, heavier than all the mountains put together. When it sits on Being, the Being that is the womb of the whole universe, Being cannot move*, and that is precisely the problem. The ego and what it thinks it needs to support itself are hefty, dead weight and we'll hardly budge up the mountain if we try to drag that baggage along.

To enter the wilds means to leave behind the very *mindset* of our previous life. The earlier quotation from Hosea, in which God promises to lure the soul into wilderness, is a fundamental aspect of the call. This is the same message he delivered to the Israelites when he led them from Egypt into the barrens. We may not physically leave family, home, church, job, or the other icons of our youth, but our attitudes towards our past are likely to transform at their very core. We have to become remorseless and courageous iconoclasts to free ourselves spiritually. Franciscan priest Richard Rohr spoke of discharging our *loyal soldier*, the elder son of the prodigal story. He wrote:

> We must leave home to find the real and larger home. ... The nuclear family [which Father Rohr defines as *family-of-origin stuff, local church stuff, cultural stuff, flag-and-country stuff*] has far too often been the enemy of the global family and mature spiritual seeking.[4]

All of this *stuff* represents sticking points and obstacles along the way—relationships, creeds and slogans we must release. We once pitched our tents in these places, but now it's time to pull up stakes and move on. As we say goodbye to the lifelong expectations of family and peers, who they think we are or who they think we ought to be, they may choose to take offense, call us crazy, withdraw their affection or sever whatever connection they had to us. We shouldn't be surprised if they do; we may hardly recognize ourselves once the fresh winds of fundamental change sweep through us. We are no longer sure who we are or ought to be either. Those who assumed they knew us might say we've gone off the deep end. They're right there too, of course, although they (like we) have no inkling just how deep it's going to be.

These are difficult partings, but we won't lack for human contact. We will have new companionship on our journey as we meet like-minded people going our way, although the Velcro that holds our new community together is not our thoughts about each other, but rather a shared commitment to the pilgrimage, a mutual attraction to mystery. These are selfless friendships among people who sincerely want to help each other to the summit of the mountain.

Detachment and self-denial are summed up in the Latin phrase *agere contra*—to *go against* the inclinations and wishes of the small self. This task is ritualized in religious observances like Lent and Ramadan when we fast and consciously give up things we enjoy, or take on positive activities such as works of

---

[4] Richard Rohr, *Falling Upward*, (San Francisco: Jossey-Bass, 2011), p. 84.

charity beyond our normal actions. The goal of these rituals, beyond preparation for a pending holy day or season, is to transcend our lower hungers—*transcend*, not *obliterate* them.

Surrendering one's personal desires is a practice I suspect many wives and daughters come by early, although it would hardly be voluntary or fulfilling in subservient situations. Men seem to take much longer at relinquishment, one of the downsides of living in male-dominated societies. Hopefully, we men will have opportunities to rehearse such surrender sooner, rather than later, in the trek up Mystic Mountain.

The pattern we are trying to establish through *agere contra* is a disposition of will, a habit of releasing the desires of the small self to the beneficial wishes of the true Self, which seeks only our well-being. Going against the small self may make the ego feel it has been plunged into hell, but hell often is just another name for training. The transformative goal—total nakedness, emptiness and poverty—like the call to surrender, reverberates again and again during the climb up Mystic Mountain. At the trailhead, letting go applies primarily to our links to the exterior world, but at higher levels it will apply equally to stripping our very souls, releasing everything not That-Which-Is.

Surrender represents one aspect of our groundwork. The other, the sublimation of that which remains of us, happens in parallel with this detachment. We may use a machete to clear the tangle of our attachments, but this matching step will require pruning tools. The pruning does not involve the shrubs of the forest, however. Rather, we will trim ourselves, paring away what is spiritually unproductive and thereby encouraging the fruitful growth of what medieval masters called our *faculties*. These include the mind that, with information from the senses, is interior to the body. The higher mind capable of abstraction and intuition, the mind that enabled a deaf Beethoven to compose his magnificent symphonies, is deeper still than the sensual mind. Soul or psyche, with its feelings, moods, appetites, imagination and beliefs is nested within mind, and furthest within, at the core of our being is our eternal spirit, the part of us that interacts with Divinity.

We will train and educate these aspects of ourselves through a range of spiritual practices that, once more, can entail years of patient perseverance, yet no real progress is possible without this commitment to regular (preferably daily) practice.

Practice, Practice, Practice

Aristotle observed more than 2300 years ago that *we are what we repeatedly do; excellence is not an act*, he taught, *but a habit.* Note that his emphasis is on what *we* do, which corresponds to the active phase of our journey.

The call is like a rebirth into the spiritual dimension and initiates a process meant to wean us from superficial thinking. A key goal of this process is self-knowledge, a thorough exploration of each feature of our inner landscapes, until we know them as well as the neighborhoods in which we played as children. This exploration repeatedly raises the question: *Who am I—really? Am I simply the product of all the commercials drummed into my head since childhood? Am I that person who sits in a cubicle and taps away the day on a keyboard? Am I that opposite person who parties on the weekend to release the stress of the workweek? Are either of these versions of me, or their variations, authentic?* Fortunately, the quest takes us deep beneath these superficial aspects of our persona.

Knowledge of the unbounded Love that we call *God* is the other goal of this process, and we approach both it and self-knowledge through spiritual disciplines: chanting, verbal prayer, reading sacred texts and the works of spiritual masters, reflection and meditation, our work and our service to others— all meant to lead us outside the ordinary way of thinking. Guidance from a living spiritual master can aid this process, although it takes discernment to distinguish true teachers committed to transforming students from those who are merely in the guru *business*—not an easy task in this beginner stage. If we do look to teachers for guidance, we will recognize their validity in their willingness to serve. We also must be convinced that they are not operating from the very levels we hope to abandon. Ken Wilbur offers a caveat that we can apply to potential gurus as well as to keep ourselves humble in the course of spiritual progress:

Some individuals—including spiritual teachers—may be highly evolved in certain capacities (such as meditative awareness or cognitive brilliance) and yet demonstrate poor (or even pathological) development in other streams, such as the psychosexual or interpersonal.[5]

Our humanity stalks us down all our days on earth.

Practices, while they are meant to awaken our awareness to the sacred within us and pave the way for breakthroughs to ascending levels of this awareness, also link the material to the spiritual when we carry them into our normal routines. They do not negate or destroy the material, but rather elevate it, incorporate it into the journey, so that every aspect of the physical world becomes a helper on the way and our external actions become consistent with our inner transformation. These disciplines join body, mind and soul, ideas, activities and concerns to spirit, again with transfiguration as the goal. Spirituality does not consist solely of lofty thoughts and feelings, but includes the ordinary events and habits of the day-to-day. In this sense, practice includes the most normal behaviors, eating and breathing and sleeping, performed with deepened awareness. Warm cleansing showers, working in the garden or at a job, creating works of art—every activity, when it springs from the sacred sense within us, bonds us more tightly to the holy. The most profane or commonplace act can be made sacred, depending on how we carry it out. Similarly, no word or action is wasted effort except when we speak or act to no real purpose.

Practice also includes the exercise of virtues such as patience, generosity, gentleness and compassion, both towards ourselves and others. The journey requires faith, courage and trust as well. Through these exercises we still our minds and emotions, weaken the cords of attachments and addictions, and potentially can renovate our lives until they are sanctified and approach the holiness of God. Through persistence in our practice, we allow miracles of grace to occur. We may not be members of a monastic community, but we can emulate the

---

[5] Ken Wilbur, *A Theory of Everything*, (Boston: Shambhala Publications, 2000), p. 45

spirit of Benedict who urges his spiritual sons, *Ora et Labora*, Pray and Work, and make our labors single-minded—directed to God alone. A Buddhist monk or nun would summarize work performed in this spirit as right action, right livelihood and right effort. A Jew would call it *kiddush hashem*, sanctifying God's Name through our everyday actions.

Once we recognize Love's role in our lives, we don't break faith with It. Practice is our promise to rendezvous with God each day in a spirit of childlike trust, to rededicate ourselves to the way as we rise each morning, and to return as often as we can, despite the distractions of the day, to awareness of divine presence within and around us. It is our refusal to take any aspect of our journey for granted that nurtures the contemplative attitude towards our world and our daily lives.

The high road

When we set out on this pilgrimage, we commit to take the high road in our decision-making, to live in right intention insofar as we are able, even at the level of our thoughts and fantasies. A choice to act from the highest aspect of ourselves in our dealings with others is one way to avoid catering to the small self. This won't always be easy. As Augustine noted, even to desire God or to set out on the mystic way requires the inspiration of Grace. Following the high road also can lead to misunderstandings. *Do not be surprised if the world hates you*, Jesus warned his followers. We are always human, but not always humane. We will always encounter those who prefer the low road, con artists and charlatans stuck in money issues, angry types itching to defend their prejudices, narcissists who feel the world should revolve around them (instead of us)—those we tend to dismiss as the sad, unaware segment of humanity although most of us likely have been hoist on that petard at some points in our lives.

A large part of our interwoven family, unfortunately, is still submerged in dualism and fear, brainwashed by network news and political sloganeering that pour on anxiety. Be afraid, be very afraid—of that other country, of my political opponent, of the latest incurable pandemic, of the approaching storm, of cancer, that other race, gang bangers, acne, bad breath, e-coli, of buying the wrong car or missing the next party, of rejection, losing face, embarrassment. So many reasons to worry, so many reminders that we absolutely need to free ourselves from this delusional madness. This is when we lead the small self to the quietest corner of our inner shrine, there to prostrate before Ultimate Being and beg for divine mercy and support.

On the high road, we will discover that love and compassion come more easily, that diversions and turbulence are easier to dismiss. We will still encounter tests intended to strengthen us and invite us (frequently) to reexamine our commitment. Despite traveling the high road, we still have to confront a stubborn, reflexive resistance to unreserved commitment, amplified by the daily distractions in our lives. We must ask ourselves, *Am I trying to keep a foot in each world? Would I rather think and read about the spiritual life than live it? Do I use study about prayer as a way to avoid praying?* Learning is, or ought to be, a gateway to our interior and a contemplative approach to life.

Yet we have so many things we want to do, so many plans and worries about what lies ahead, that we usually do not notice God waiting patiently right before us. Used to scurrying like sanderlings dodging sea foam on a beach, we ignore the awe-inspiring ocean of Grace, satisfied with the meager gifts, the tiny crabs and insects, left in its wake.

Moreover, as the ego weakens, we will discover that it becomes more subtle in its attempts to preserve itself. It is a fierce survivor and like a jealous, jilted lover, it will do all in its power to impede our redirection, inviting us to various expressions of spiritual infidelity. It would live in its body forever if it could. At its most subversive, the ego will try to take credit for any progress we may have noticed (or imagined) on our way—even though the heart understands that each gain is a gift of Grace. Or it may try to convince us that our spanking new, spiritual self is superior to the nonspiritual self of that other person still slouching along the low road. What better place for the ego to conceal itself than at the heart of our spirituality, in our devotions, our acts of charity, in our spiritual studies, all in the name of the way? Thus, even the ascent of Mystic Mountain can become an ego trip.

Spiritual pride is the formal name for these gyrations. See them for what they are and pray humbly and sincerely not to be unfaithful to the task, to the graces granted us, and to continue trusting Love to guide our footsteps homeward. Only with God's help can we avoid such pitfalls.

Verbal prayer

In the beginning is the word. Yes, words do limit and, in that sense, violate the objects they describe. Once we attach a name to something, we reduce the range of its possibilities. But words also can concentrate our initial efforts, awakening our consciousness and reinforcing our commitment. Later, when we approach the ineffable and the brilliance of Spirit eclipses the lesser light of our minds, words lose their significance and we grow still, but this is where we begin.

When Jesus' disciples asked, *Lord, teach us to pray*, he replied by giving them verbal prayer. He did not teach them meditation or contemplation. Spiritually, they were still toddlers and would not be ready for wordless (and thought-less) prayer until Spirit descended on them at Pentecost.

> We don't teach meditation to the young monks. They are not ready for it until they stop slamming doors.
> —Thich Nhat Hanh

Prayer, then, is initially verbal, whether spoken aloud or silently in our minds. It may be occasional in the beginning, but ideally will evolve into a routine, much as cloistered Christians intone the canonical hours or Hindus fill their day with Sanskrit chants. As we develop a clearly visible prayer schedule, we will find that others will respect the time we set aside and support us in our efforts. They may even want to join us. At times, particularly in a group setting, prayer may overflow into spiritual fervor expressed through song or dance or musical instruments. This is the path of *bhakti yoga* in Hinduism, *union* through *devotion*. We also see this outpouring of zeal in the Sufi whirling dervishes, in Hindu and Jewish festival processions, or the worship ceremonies of charismatic Christians.

> Praise God in his holy place ...
> Praise him with fanfare of trumpet.

> Praise him with harp and lyre.
> Praise him with tambourines and dancing.
> Praise him with strings and pipes.
> Praise him with the clamor of cymbals.
> —Psalm 150

Makes you want to break out the finger castanets and start twirling or dance in rings of fire like the disciples of the Baal Shem Tov.

The pilgrim also enters the "first dwelling" of Teresa of Avila's *Interior Castle* through prayer, beginning with verbal prayer, and most importantly for her the Lord's Prayer that Jesus taught to his followers. Teresa saw that particular prayer as a roadmap for the entire spiritual journey, as she explained to her nuns in *The Way of Perfection*. Not surprisingly, Teresa warned that distractions and day-to-day concerns (*reptiles* she called them) will follow us into this first dwelling. We're still new at spirituality and usually forget to close the door behind us. Even this early on, though, we become more conscious of our shortcomings, and more pained by them because of heightened self-awareness and our growing love for God, but Teresa reassured her Carmelite daughters that God will show us extra mercy at this stage. That-Which-Is knows what we're up against. It *remembers that we are dust* (Psalm 103), and divine Love does not waver.

A point to consider here (and throughout our journey) is that *nothing we do can make God love us less; nothing we do can make God love us more.* God's Love, of its nature, must be infinite and unconditional, or God would not be God. Ultimate Being demonstrated that Love when It created us, and again now that It has entered our consciousness, inviting us to leave the crowd and grow in intimacy with It. God sends divine Grace *to help us change* our lives; Love does not happen after-the-fact, *because we have changed*. This is not good news, of course, for those in the fire and brimstone business, who make a career of orchestrating sin and guilt or warning that we must live in constant dread of God's vengeance.

> You will not be punished for your anger.
> You will be punished *by* your anger.
> —The Buddha

We need to treat ourselves with forbearance and patience. We can't calm our minds immediately or through force. The unstable mind is, in fact, likely to become more irritated as a result of efforts to restrain it. Shooing a hornet off your arm with a wave of the hand hurts a lot less than trying to snatch it in your fist!

Perseverance, humility, a sense of humor and pure intention are all needed from the outset of the journey. By *pure intention* I mean *desiring* to align our will and actions with the will of God as we understand it, with the guidance of our higher Self or higher Mind, even though we often backslide in our efforts. These initial failures and distractions in prayer are not overwhelming problems, certainly not causes for scruples or self-flagellation, so long as our motive is sincere. They are simply (persistent) reminders of the work we still have to do.

We all know how it goes: we kneel, or sit or stand to pray, hands folded, eyes closed or lifted skyward, when a mosquito buzzes by one ear and the neighbor down the hill revs up her motorcycle. Somewhere in the house a door opens and closes and footsteps pad down the hall. We continue on with words that seemingly speak to God, but our focus has flown completely out the window, and we're thinking that the motorcycle has the characteristic rumble of a Harley. Maybe we're remembering this morning's breakfast or wondering what's for lunch, we worry about something that may (or may not) happen next week, a chore or shopping that we forgot to do, or find ourselves sidetracked by some other whimsy fluttering like a butterfly through the brain. Our prayer is in shambles—but our underlying intention need not be. Don't believe the old cliché about the road to hell. We're still on the high way!

Spiritual reading

On a quieter note, in spiritual reading (called *lectio divina* in medieval guides), we are privileged to explore sacred texts and the works of those who have journeyed ahead of us. Meaningful reading has always been a special delight of mine and how I would happily pass most of my time. Old rockin' chair's gonna get me, and I'll be fine with that as long as I have an enlightening tome nearby, to spend my days like Thomas à Kempis with *a little book in a little corner.*

Through their writings and sermons, masters and guides and teachers extend a hand to us, both to share what they've discovered and to lead us forward. Spiritual reading, like prayer, also keeps us mindful of God's presence. When we pray, we speak to God; when we read, God speaks to us. Thus begins the dialog that eventually becomes one voice, one speaking, and that's when we finally will set aside our books.

Those of us who grew up in a particular religious tradition are likely familiar with the scriptures that make up its foundation. We also have available a plethora of commentaries on those texts, as well as commentaries on the commentaries, and so on. Each level removed from the original message can weaken its impact, unfortunately, especially if the author is caught up in egoic detours or focused more on his or her personal message than the meaning of the scripture.

A Hindu tale tells of a cook who invited his friend to enjoy a delicious duck soup. His guest was greatly impressed and went away singing the praises of the meal.

The next evening a man arrived at the door saying "I am a friend of your friend, and wondered if I might try a bowl of your wonderful soup?" The cook didn't know what to think, but added a bit of water to the duck soup to be sure he had enough and gave it to the man, who also went away satisfied.

This continued for five days, until another person knocked at the door and introduced himself as "a friend of the friend of the friend of the friend of your friend" and also asked to try the now-famous soup. By this time, however, the poor cook had been forced to water it down so often that it was nearly tasteless.

The visitor spat out the first sip and complained, "This can't be the duck soup I've heard praised so highly."

"Alas," apologized the cook, "all I had left to serve you was the soup of the soup of the soup of the soup of my soup."

It's little wonder that Francis of Assisi warned his followers against scholarship and told them to read nothing but the scriptures. The only priest in his original cadre, friar Pietro, had been a priest before he joined Francis, which was how the little poor man preferred it. He didn't want his friars bogged down in scholasticism and theology and other studies for the priesthood.

If you surround a teacher with a hundred followers, you likely will get a hundred interpretations of the master's message. Over many iterations and the curious workings of institutions, these can evolve into total distortions, turning the original words into the very opposite of their first intent. All the great spiritual masters, for example, spoke to their disciples of peace and love and respect for all beings, yet the religions founded in their names degenerated into periodic bloodbaths—whether torturing and burning "heretics" or waging wars of "truth" against each other in the name of God. Governments do the same with high-sounding patriotic slogans. *Praise the Lord and pass the ammunition*!

Stay as close to the original lessons as you can. It's true that even these can go astray through many iterations, translations and, very likely, even edits. The inspiration of Spirit, however, can use these words to ignite spontaneous reflection on the deeper meaning of these texts and a brief prayer for divine enlightenment is a good way to begin *lection divina*.

Spiritual reading can also open entries into the forms of meditation typical of this early stage. Reflecting on a particular passage is the practice of *lectio divina* as intended. The mind moves naturally back and forth between reading and rumination without regard to time, in an almost trancelike state of mind.

> I set about reading *The Philokalia*. ... and this reading kindled in my soul a zealous desire to make what I had read a matter of practical experience. I saw clearly what interior prayer means, how it is to be reached, and what

the fruits of it are, how it fills one's heart and soul with delight.[6]

Spiritual study is the second of the four great "yogas," or Hindu pathways to union. I mentioned *Bhakti yoga* earlier. *Jnana yoga* seeks union with God via the path of *wisdom*. It emphasizes reason and abstract thought, leading the seeker to a point of spiritual discernment. The latter enables him or her to separate appearances and illusion from true Reality or, put another way, to pierce through dualism to oneness.

Meditation, reflection and recollection

A student of the Zen master, Shunryu Suzuki Roshi, bemoaned the flow of thought that distracted his meditation. The Roshi, whether bemused or puzzled, asked the young man in turn, *is there some problem with thinking?*

The form of meditation we exercise at this stage actually *requires* thought and imagination, insight and reflection. It is not to be understood in the Eastern sense, where the term *meditation* generally refers to the non-reflective discipline we in the West call *contemplation*. The beginner's practice is also called *discursive* or *analytical meditation*, and involves focused attention on a specific topic. This might be, for example, an incident in the life of a saint, a line from a sacred text or prayer, or sermon. Quite often, as mentioned, we find ourselves reflecting naturally in the course of our reading, when we pause to ponder a line that strikes us. Discursive meditation also can include visualizations and imaginative exploration of its subject.

When we settle into meditation as a separate event apart from study, we start by reminding ourselves of God's presence, the happy thought that we are always enveloped in Love. We might sit cross-legged on a cushion if discomfort does not become a distraction from the meditation itself. Standing meditation, seated meditation and even lying down while we meditate can work too, although the latter obviously is an invitation to sleep, especially if we are tired before we start.

---

[6] R. M. French (trans), *The Way of a Pilgrim*, (New York: Harper, 1954)

Initially we may be able to focus only a short time, say fifteen minutes, but with practice an expanding sense of timelessness can extend this period. As with verbal prayer, distractions will come, but once again, we can approach them softly, simply watch them as if they were passing traffic, let them whiz through and out of our consciousness.

Discursive meditation is a gateway to deeper forms of mental prayer. It typically leads us beyond reflection into *recollection*, an active withdrawal of our senses and thoughts from our circumference, our exterior world, gathering (or collecting) them to the center of our being. Often, we accomplish this while we repeat a mantra, a word or phrase that we can synchronize with our breathing to aid our concentration and remind us that we are in the divine presence. In some cases, a student receives the mantra from a teacher; most often, however, the word or phrase, like our particular spiritual path, chooses us.

I've found that the two-syllable name *Yahweh* or the four-syllable Yod-Hey-Vah-Hey (YHWH) are perfect for such centered breathing, as are the *so-ham* and *tat-tvam-asi* phrases mentioned earlier. An Orthodox Christian might wish to repeat the *Jesus Prayer* or a shortened version. The full prayer is *Lord Jesus Christ, Son of God, have mercy on me a sinner*, which might be abbreviated to *Lord Jesus Christ, have mercy on me* or to the Greek *Christe Eléison*. The last is most easily coordinated with the breath. The prayer for divine mercy is especially potent for "mercy" covers all the bases, everything we possibly could need wrapped up in a single gift.

As our awareness of God's presence within us becomes more acute, we may experience an inner stillness and focus unlike anything we've been able to achieve on our own. This is our first taste of *infused* prayer. Typically, our initial experience of *infused recollection* is fleeting, but it does prod our determination to continue practicing active recollection.

We need not concern ourselves with consolation or dryness during verbal prayer or recollection. We need not "feel good" about either practice, or feel anything in particular. While we try to remain in God's presence in meekness, humility and love, the ego, shaken up by our new tendencies, does not feel particularly meek or humble or in love with God. It would prefer to be left alone and allowed to return to its old ways. During these first steps, however, it is enough for the new and growing *us* that we *want* to be humble and *want* to be in love with the divine. It is the road to *nirvana* that is paved with good intentions.

Such desiring is all God expects or asks from us for now. Showing up consistently with commitment and God-centered intention is the work Love assigns novice seekers. We can be fairly certain we're on track as our practice becomes habitual if we begin to experience abiding peacefulness building within us. This stillness is most noticeable when we are alone and the noise around us is hushed.

Solitude and silence

Longing for solitude and silence is a natural extension of reading and meditation. Ideally, nothing will disturb these restful activities. We know we need to leave the house to buy groceries, go to work, or meet our living needs, but we find ourselves doing so with growing reluctance. Other hubbub that once filled our days—joining friends, television, the morning paper, Sudoku or crossword puzzles, movies, ballgames, politics and gossip, telephone chatter, social-networking—hold decreasing allure for us and, in fact, become annoyances. The soul instinctively recognizes the falsity in these passing gratifications. Basil the Great came to the same realization centuries ago:

> The eye cannot appreciate an object set before it if it is perpetually restless, glancing here, there and everywhere. No more can our mind's eye apprehend the Truth with any clarity if it is distracted by a thousand worldly concerns.

Before we can hope to counter the turmoil of the world with healing, peace and serenity, we must solidify them in private. All spiritual teachers encourage solitude and silence as two of the preeminent means to further inner growth and we soon discover they are essential companions. We may find ourselves seeking out a solitary grove, quiet ponds where mist softens the sharp contours of overarching pines, an empty church or isolated Zen garden, any place where we can reflect freely. A particular treat is taking time away from the chaos for several days to visit a dedicated sanctuary, take part in a guided or silent retreat, or to join a pilgrimage to some holy shrine. My own history and geography lead me to a Trappist monastery in northern Oregon where the silence is so palpable I can practically gather it up in my palms, but the availability of such sacred havens is virtually unlimited. They can be summoned up with a few clicks on the Internet. We could not wish for more perfect settings in which to review our lives and kick-start the spirit's renovation.

Solitude and silence are particularly important at the beginning of the way. We will need to bring what we learn in tranquility into situations that once upset us, to shed insight on all sorts of familiar and unfamiliar settings. We shouldn't be surprised to find ourselves suddenly rapt in silence in the most ordinary surroundings, perhaps while admiring bins of colorful fruit in a grocery store. The puzzled clerk bustles past, asks if we need help, to which we shake our head, no. His question only reinforces the cocoon of stillness as does an unsought thought from Rûmî: *Wherever you stand, be the soul of that place.* Time and body come to complete rest and we realize that we have connected with something outside the clockwork. Silence, we discover in such moments, is not an absence, a lack, but a link to profound presence and communication. Breaking silence, on the contrary, can limit us and center us once more on ourselves and the ego's opinions. Meister Eckhart said: *I like best those things in which I see most clearly the likeness of God. Nothing in all creation is so like God as stillness.*

Solitude and silence, like our other practices, lead to a deepening of prayer. In the private space within our hearts, the innermost secret sanctum, our *holy of holies*, we not only shut the door on the chaotic outside world, but also on our noisy or idle minds. Eventually we will learn simply to rest in God, to listen like the prophet Elijah for the voice within the stillness (1 Kings 19:11-14):

> There came a mighty wind, so strong it tore the mountains and shattered the rocks before Yahweh, But Yahweh was not in the wind. After the wind came an earthquake. But Yahweh was not in the earthquake. After the earthquake

came a fire. But Yahweh was not in the fire. And after the fire there came the sound of a gentle breeze. And when Elijah heard this, he covered his face with his cloak and went out and stood at the entrance of the cave. Then a voice came to him ...

The voice within the stillness is that non-audible sound the Islamic tradition calls *Hu*, the basic energy vibrating through the universe. *Hu* is also another name for the Self or for God, which adds another dimension to the word *Hu-man*, emphasizing the link between us and the Divine.

In the frenzied, fearful, unaware period of our lives, to be alone might have seemed synonymous with loneliness or insecurity or boredom. Anyone who needs a lot of reinforcement or affection from others may learn the hard way how quickly others forget us when we retreat into solitude. Yet when we open ourselves in this solitude, allow God's Being to enter our voluntary isolation, we begin to sense that we are loved more attentively than any friend ever could.

As we set out across our inner landscapes, we begin to welcome each opportunity to leave the crowded marketplace and make room for the Godhead in our lives. We can stand outside the turmoil of the mighty wind, the earthquake and the fire, and look with serenity (and awe) at what is real. Having silenced the inner barrage, we also can develop what wisdom traditions call *witness consciousness*. In stillness, as spectators, we can observe our thoughts, actions and reactions, emotions, inner critic, doubts, fears and fantasies in minute detail—in slow motion as it were, like a fisherman eyeing a trout suspended just below the surface of a clear, quiet stream. This witness stance is crucial to greater self-knowledge.

Self-knowledge

The unexamined life is not worth living, taught Socrates, and this is doubly true of the soul on a spiritual walkabout. *Know thyself!* Before we can discover who we *really* are, however, we must come to terms with the false identities and coping tools we've created to survive our earlier years. We need to review the larger pattern in our time here, try to see the divine design in all that has transpired in our lives until now.

Where was God at that time of our lives? Was the impulse toward spirituality at all visible back then or was it buried beneath a thousand other concerns? Where were the points of basic choice in our lives that determined whether we took a constructive or destructive path from thence forward? Sometimes the only way to get back to that point of a fundamental option if the choice was destructive is to let go of everything that has happened since, get back to square one.

The answer to the question *Who am I?* will go through much shape-shifting as our constricted personas wane and our true Self emerges. We begin with a reality check, our world *as it is*—and ourselves *as we are*—at this very hour, with no judgments, no agendas, no fixed attitudes.

A runner friend in his mid-seventies once mentioned how, after a race, he'd told his wife he would jog the several miles back to their home and she could follow in the truck after she'd finished her errands in town. A half-hour later, as he was heading up an incline, he heard the familiar motor chugging from behind. He straightened, threw out his chest, lifted his knees a bit higher and pumped his arms as she passed. When he finally reached the house, he asked, "How did I look back there?" She replied matter-of-factly, "Like a little old man running up a hill."

Nothing special, this ordinary property we share with our fellow beings. Once we let go of our need to be exceptional—the odd notion that the illusory ego we have created is somehow superior to the illusory ego created by that other fellow—we are on the road toward wholeness. To borrow a Native American image, we can move forward with the *clear heart* of candid clarity, with an *open heart* that can be vulnerable for the sake of growth, with the *full heart* of unreserved commitment, and the *strong heart* of courage.

How do we gain self-knowledge? One way is the the life review just mentioned. In addition, as we still our minds through silence and meditation, we become better able to employ the witness consciousness—simply watching what drives our actions, thoughts, imagination, and memories—without attachment or judgment. We also witness everything else happening in our environment, every sensation that strikes our sight, hearing, touch, smell and taste, observing our ego in its total context. We participate in our lives like playgoers at a theater, taking in the drama, but without trying to control the actors.

This leads to ongoing interrogation. *Where did that idea come from? What inside me made me react like that? What triggered last night's dream? Why is this memory upsetting?* Questions such as these lead to greater honesty about our motives and who we really are. The sincere seeker consequently can *adjust* his or her decision-making guided by right intention and honorable behavior—not an easy process, but an integral step in our pilgrim's progress.

Through our actions and our reactions, then, we begin to see ourselves as we truly are. Emotional swings may seem like obstacles to inner peace, but they are actually learning opportunities, triggers that help us understand where we are at present and what illusions we've stumbled into over the years to reach this place. They are the first steps in freeing ourselves from ego and its lifetime of conditioning.

On the path to enlightenment we will be asked to confront and transcend our emotions, our anger, fear, jealousy, pride, desire, and mental confusion. We also will expose the mental gymnastics we've used to rationalize our outbursts. Paying attention to what pushes our buttons is the best indicator of the work we need to do.

The semi-legendary mystic and poet Milarepa wrote in the eleventh century:

> See demons as demons: that is the danger.
> Know that they are powerless: that is the way.
> Understand them for what they are: that is deliverance.
> Recognize them as your father and mother: that is their end.
> Realize that they are creations of the mind:
> they become its glory.
> When these truths are known, all is liberation.[7]

---

[7] *The Hundred Thousand Songs of Milarepa*, cited in Danielle and Olivier Föllmi, *Offerings*, (New York: Stewart, Tabori & Chang, 2003)

Once we see our passions, fears and inner contradictions as our father and mother (that is, as friends and teachers), we can welcome and embrace them. They expose our complexity, but that does not mean, for example, that one side of a contradiction must be "wrong" or must be purged from our consciousness. Better it is to hold and absorb both sides—the *others* we fear *within* us—cradle them gently and ask what they wish to teach us. They are not demons before whom we must cower. In modern parlance, they would be called our shadows, the aspects we hide from ourselves and the outside world, and, yes, embracing our shadows *is* necessary to our transformation, part of becoming whole persons. We must learn to navigate the dark as well as the light regions of our inner landscape just as the roots of a mighty oak navigate slabs of shale and other obstacles to seek out nutrients in the dark earth beneath the sunlit surface.

The more we complicate our lives, the more wound up and at war we are inside ourselves, the more estranged we will be from inner calm and freedom. This is stating the obvious, of course! A common characteristic in enlightened people I have known is their transparency and simplicity. Loving God with all their heart, soul, mind and strength, they enjoy a freedom that liberates them from concern about the small details that harass most of us to the brink of submission. They are no longer confused by the complexities of their personas, but recognize the different aspects of their personalities as outliers, gatekeepers ushering them into the single immensity beyond contradictions. They have accepted everything within them as part of their total being, just as everything in the universe is part of the wholeness of creation. Their vision of oneness shapes their view of their individuality.

The more we place our shadows in their proper, nondualistic perspective, the more we can accept and respect ourselves as we are and others as they are, the freer we will be of our *demons*, and the more fully Love can expand within us. *Blessed are your contradictions*, John O'Donohue said, *for more surely than any of your ideas, they will set you free.* He added, quite beautifully,

> When we befriend the twilight side of the heart, we discover a surer tranquility where the darkness and the brightness of our lives dwell together. ... We learn to befriend our complexity and see the dance of opposition within us not as a negative or destructive thing, but as an invitation to a creative adventure. The true beauty of a person glimmers like a slow twilight where the full force of each color comes alive and yet blends with the others to create a new light.[8]

That's the ideal, the good news. Shadow work, as it turns out, is also endless. Self-knowledge and self-transfiguration are literally the work of a lifetime, maybe of many lifetimes. We will always have buttons someone can push. Many of us spend our adult years trying to undo the damage of dysfunctional childhoods. Depending on our starting point, where we stand or are mired when we hear the divine invitation, deconstructing our false egos may demand decades of effort and perseverance, many falls as we trip over the roots and rocks in the path and much scrambling to regain our footing. On the positive side, we are here to learn and we do, in all honesty, learn more from our mistakes than from our successes. We are dealing with accumulated layers of attachment, buried impulses, destructive habits and a lifetime of dualistic thinking. We would love to walk in stillness, but something within us rebels, tossing up conflicts and confusion to trip us up. The tenacious ego restraining the limitless spirit is like a hard, marble sarcophagus that requires endless chipping and sanding and the slow erosion of Grace before it will release the captive within.

So self-observation applies to subconscious levels, to our hidden angst as well as our obvious behavior. Even after we feel we are interiorly composed and have made some bit of progress, we may find ourselves troubled by recurring nightmares that expose deeply-buried terrors needing attention—fears of becoming lost in life, of growing vulnerability or ill-health as we age, of violence from outside invading our inner peace. But during *lucid* dreaming we can

---

[8] John O'Donohue, *Beauty* (New York: HarperCollins, 2004), p. 39.

also witness such fantasies just as we do our conscious thoughts. We can remind ourselves even in sleep that they are figments of the mind like the demons in Milarepa's poem, that we created this movie and can therefore rewind it and give it a more satisfying resolution.

Dreams then become but another opportunity for self-knowledge and inner work. Unpeeling these seemingly limitless layers of the human mind is like stripping an artichoke. Leaf-by-leaf we work our way through layers of protective armor towards the tasty choke at its heart, but each leaf also has its savory bit at its tip, and those hints of the ultimate reward at the center are what keep us peeling.

The creations of the mind are as plentiful and ephemeral as dust motes dancing in a sunray. Perhaps this is why the greatest saints could claim to be the greatest "sinners." The closer we are to the Light, the more "dust," the more troubling creations of our minds, we see. Self-awareness, acknowledging ourselves as we are, coupled with a growing awareness of God's grandeur, cannot but leave us humbled, which is a wonderful thing. God hides the holy within our flaws. Humility is absolutely needed to continue our search for the sacred. Without it, we will never surrender entirely to Love, but instead will remain steadfastly reliant on our own efforts. Without it, we might forget to remove our sandals when we find ourselves standing on holy ground.

In this long process of self-observation and questioning, we inevitably will question *who it is that is doing the witnessing*, who is the onlooker peeking behind our stage masks? What Mind is plumbing the thoughts of our small minds? And is there something deeper yet that watches the witness at work?

The observer obviously is not an aspect of our personas, which are, rather, the objects it watches, and which become less real the longer and more closely we study them. The watching entity stands apart from the illusory self. The witness is, in fact, the higher Self that knows, and knows that it knows, not the small self that is known. The higher Self helps us recognize reality by simply noting what *is* in our world, what *is* in our behavior, *as* it is. Thus, the greatest knowledge—the wisdom that surpasses understanding derived from the senses or reason—is the infused knowledge of the subject, the "I" that knows, versus the object, the "I" which is known. It is that part of us that simultaneously *knows* and *is*. Once we recognize who the witness is, we understand also that the more we exercise it, the greater will be its influence in our lives.

Ultimately, self-reflection leads to reflection on death, our eventual destination and a topic that spiritual guidebooks universally recommend for discursive meditation. We will look more closely at death in the final chapter of this book, but it's both disturbing and liberating to realize in the course of our self-observation that our physical selves, all the facts stored in our memory banks, along with our honors and achievements, pains and joys, gains, losses, beliefs and prejudices will vanish with our last breath and will come down to no more than *sound and fury signifying nothing*. For example, I do well at the board game *Trivial Pursuit*, but someday the memory that recalls who first climbed Mount Everest, ran the four-minute mile or landed on the moon will shut down permanently through death or dementia and my lifelong accumulation of trifling facts will cease to be. Perhaps authors write and artists paint or sculpt so some part of their minds-at-work will outlive them, as their legacy to their children or the world. On the other hand, when Thomas Aquinas gave up writing with his *Summa Theologica* still unfinished, he explained to Brother Reginald, *All this is straw compared to what has been revealed to me.*

In any case, life in those final breaths will come down, not to the list of things we knew here or did here or accumulated here, but to the awareness that propelled us through our years. It is not a beloved pet we release to death, but our bodies and minds and our cherished egos, the small selves we inhabited or that inhabited us for this eyeblink we call a lifetime. He who dies with the most toys does not win—or lose. He just dies.

Musing on mortality opens a portal for us, a glimpse into another Reality. We are forced to admit that we are not, all said and done, human forms and intellects dwelling in time and space. Everything attached to that illusion evaporates when we pass. Once we accept this, we come closer to *experiencing*, not just grasping intellectually, the awareness that we are instead eternal, spiritual beings hanging out for a time in physical shells.

Dealing with dualism

> The unenlightened man sees a difference,
> but the enlightened man does not.
> —Zen teaching

> It isn't a small world, but there are many ways of dividing it into small parts. Reason looks for two, then arranges it from there.
> —Lyn Hejinian

Mystics in the course of their journey undergo a transformation in which they discover that they, God and all being are one. Even within themselves, apparent separation of the faculties comes together. The highest of these, the human spirit, is the flashpoint where we and the One Only Spirit meet, the Spirit of Love that in turn searches out the depths of God (1 Corinthians 2:10). At the level of spirit we touch and merge and are leavened by that union. This is our true and timeless Self which unites with the Source behind all that is.

John of the Cross called union with all things and all things in God, *the most noble and sublime state attainable in this life.* In his view, becoming one with the One, discovering who we truly are and always have been, is quite simply the purpose behind our existence on this plane, the answer to that question, *Why, I?* Distinctions lose their hold on us and those who attain to union with Divinity share a profound love and respect for all beings. No matter how dire the circumstances of their temporal forms, a spirit of joy and peace free of fear and anxiety saturates their being.

Conversely, viewing the world dualistically, in terms of difference and separation, raises our level of apprehension. Chronic dread of the "other"—both within us and without— triggers this disorder. The shadow work mentioned earlier, the belief that a wall divides our conscious and subconscious minds, added to the belief that our souls and minds and bodies are disparate entities, are but two of many forms of dualism we must confront on our journey. Our sense that there is any time but *now,* or any place but *here,* only contributes to the confusion. *The ultimate dualism, however, the major obstacle to our enlightenment, as I mentioned earlier, is our belief that we or anything else in our universe are separate from God.* Divinity manifests in myriad forms, yet bonds and permeates all.

Money is not the root of all evil. Dualistic thinking, the illusion that any separation can exist within God, is. It is the radical rot behind every harmful thought or action, the source of all wars and violence, of nationalism, racism, claims of superiority, feelings of inferiority, religious intolerance, fear, paranoia, insecurity, unhealthy competition, lack of cooperation and charity, hoarding and greed (there's the *money* part), abuse in all its devastating displays ... the list could go on to include every instance where we exploit those we think of as *others*. Matthew Fox observed that *only the human personality is capable of imagining and acting out a division between God and us, between others and us. ... If we would let creation be, all things would teach us their common love of God. There is no escaping our unity with God and all things. The only way out is nothingness itself, for outside God there is nothing but nothing.*[9] To enter God, to simply *be* and *let be*, we must let go of dualism.

The concept of dualism was introduced into western culture in our version of the creation story—when Adam and Eve ate of the tree of knowledge of good and evil (3:1-19). Sadly, Pema Chödrön has noted, *until we stop clinging to the concept of good and evil, the world will continue to manifest as friendly goddesses and harmful demons.* Conversely, *non*dualistic thinking, letting go of our notions of right or wrong, sacred and profane, temporal and eternal, internal and external, me and thee, is a sure benchmark of spiritual progress. Embracing contradiction, blessing our enemies without as well as the enemy within, learning from those we once barred from our world physically or mentally or emotionally, bit-by-bit loosens the hold of dualism on our minds.

---

[9] Mathew Fox, *Breakthrough: Meister Eckhart's Creation Spirituality*, (Garden City: Image Books, 1980), p. 539

> "I" and "you" are the veil
> Between heaven and earth.
> —Shabistari

Artists from poets to designers of *merz bild*—collages—describe their work as the pulling together of disparate elements, from which emerges a surprising spirituality. And so it goes with our interior work. Jesus taught: *You have heard it said: You must love your neighbor and hate your enemy, but I say this to you, love your enemies, do good to those who hate you, and pray for those who persecute you and treat you badly. In this way you will be children of your Father in heaven, for he causes his sun to rise on the unjust as well as the just, and his rain to fall on the honest and dishonest alike. ... Be perfect just as your heavenly Father is perfect* (Matthew 5:43-46, 48). The vision of Oneness gathers within it the multiplicity of all creation, sees it as a whole rather than as a collection of parts, in its single *being* rather than in its endless, ever-changing, *becoming*. Richard Rohr summed up John Duns Scotus' teaching on Oneness thus:

> [He] taught that the opposite of good was not bad, but nonbeing itself. The opposite of truth was not falsity, but nonbeing itself. The opposite of unity was not multiplicity, but nonbeing itself. All opposites are ... contained within pure being.[10]

An object or a concept or anything else that lies within the province of creation must be contained within the totality of pure Being. Otherwise, it could not exist.

Each time we close some separation in our minds, restoring it to its original accord, we gain a truer view of the universe. And we can do so even in the active stage of the spiritual journey. Before we began to practice mindfulness, we probably assumed we were immersed in a stew of multiplicity, but as we change our perspective and slow our perceptions, inner and outer distinctions begin to blur.

---

[10] Richard Rohr, *Immortal Diamond*, (San Francisco: Jossey-Bass, 2012), p. 220

We can call on the witness to bring conflicts to light and embrace these seeming contradictions. Moreover, as meditation becomes less intellectual and evolves into wordless gazing, it little-by-little refines the egoic mind and exposes its illusions, including its sense of separation from the rest of creation. It loosens our identification with the small self and with lower levels of awareness. We begin to erase artificial boundaries such as the line between our personas and their shadows. Ultimate Being washes over all, coating male and female, Asian, African and Hispanic, Jew, Hindu and Muslim with the same beneficent Being. How can we hate or wish to harm aspects of our own Self once we've experienced such togetherness? Violence, conflict based on *us versus them*, is displayed in all its absurdity. No longer can we bring suffering into the world—either by offending or, just as importantly, by taking offense.

There is a game I like to play when dealing with dualism. I raise each pair of "opposites" to the next higher level of consciousness where they invariably merge. The movement from duality to unity occurs as a series of ever-higher groupings. For example, Marguerite Porete's *Mirror of Simple Souls* distinguished between *Holy Church the Little* (the institutional Church) and *Holy Church the Great* (the mystical gathering of souls united in God). At a higher level these two merge into one Holy Church, in her case the Roman Catholic Church of the Middle Ages. This and other Christian Churches at the next level merge with all formal religions (Judaism, Islam, Hinduism, Buddhism, Taoism, etc.), then with the total body of spiritual seekers, formal and informal. Seekers and nonseekers then constitute the entire human race, which then merges with all other creatures at the next level and with all forms of creation further up. When you reach the level of the created and the uncreated, or the visible and invisible universe, or the *before creation* and *after creation*, the final level is the Godhead, the Ein Sof, the one existent that shines through every form of being from behind every form of being. You might try this exercise yourself, starting with opposites such as *friends* and *enemies*, qualities such as *active* and *passive* or (gulp) the political hot buttons of *liberal* and *conservative*. Ultimately, every dualism is subsumed into the One.

I chose the example of Marguerite and her two Churches intentionally because the question often arises, what is the role of formal religion, of *Holy Church the Little*, in the mystic journey? Marguerite, of course, was burned at the stake for her comments and critics might claim that that is still the role of official religion. But the question remains, do the institutional churches have a part to play in the growth of the mystic life?

Formal Religion and the Mystic Way

You need not carry the raft after you've crossed the river.
—Buddha

Every day people are straying away from the church and going back to God.
—Lenny Bruce

The flatlands leading to Mystic Mountain are pocked with the structures of formal religion. Like the institutions of government, education, finance, industry and war, like the criminal and justice systems, organized religion has been systematized to regulate our exterior lives and codify those norms of "goodness" that stabilize us as a society. It offers a soothing embellishment to the well-ordered life, for seldom will we hear a sermon meant to shake us from our comfort zones. It also offers canned answers to help us deal with our fear of death and the puzzling "bad" things that happen to "good" people (like us).

When he described the phases of spiritual progress, Augustine said *the third stage is reached when people more and more forsake their mothers and depart further and further from the womb*. He may have been thinking of his own mother, Monica, who had more worldly ambitions for her son than he, but the same instruction could apply to *Mother Church*, and has its parallel in the call to Abram to leave his kinsfolk and father's house.

The crux of the matter, at least from the institutional viewpoint, seems to be: Who gets to translate the voice of God? Who gets to interpret the sacred texts? The established churches would reserve this privilege to their trained professionals and dismiss (rather loudly at times) the notion of a direct relationship between God and ordinary seekers. In the history of my own country, the visionary Anne Hutchinson was expelled from the pioneer Pilgrim community and revivalist George Whitefield had a mighty tussle with his own Anglican Church over this issue. Some churches, or at least their representatives, consider *mysticism* a dirty word. Mystics don't speak the programmed language of religion. Instead of "Thou shalt *not* ... saith the Lord," they can only stammer out their own inner experience of divine Love. Think of the many mystics condemned as heretics and blasphemers because their accusers were too unenlightened or fearful to grasp the wonders they described.

It's fairly easy to take potshots at the institutions of religion, any religion, and perhaps none more than the one in which I've spent a good part of my life, Roman Catholicism. In the first years of this 21st century, the old boys in Rome seem bent on turning the church into a private, male-only, ultraconservative club. You need answers, we have them all. What we don't have is doubts or questions. Like a dutiful and ancient mare, Mother continues to plod along in her blinders, furrowing the same doctrinal rows she has ploughed for the last eight centuries, seemingly oblivious to the world evolving outside her fortified walls. She generally circles to her right because that is her nature.

Unfortunately, an eagle cannot soar, but can only hobble in circles if it severs its own left wing, flailing to lift off with its right wing only—and vice versa. God bless the fundamentalists too. Still, one must wonder whether we are hearing in recent edicts from the Vatican's Congregation for the Doctrine of the Faith (formerly known as the Inquisition) the death rattle of an increasingly irrelevant empire. My hope is that the papacy of Pope Francis will make *my concern* irrelevant.

Those among us who have attended or still attend worship services are likely well aware of the limits of institutional religion. We have come to know ourselves as God-fearing folk, but also God-loving. We understand that the *beginning* of wisdom is fear of the Lord, but have also heard the message of Love that fulfills the law (both the Mosaic law and that reintroduced into the Roman church in the Middle Ages by the scholastics). In ancient Israel, the law regulated civil and religious life, but the formation of the Sanhedrin and construction of the temple in Jerusalem eclipsed the light of the Spirit in the Jewish religion and stultified its evolution. The same could be said of the Roman church co-opted by Constantine for the purposes of empire. Spiritual dissidents like the Essenes and the Gnostics were forced underground, figuratively into the catacombs.

We can say of almost all formalized religions that organization, creation of hierarchies and power structures and fossilizing the sacred texts are the surest way to deaden the original spirit and message of their founders. The highway to heaven becomes a cul-de-sac. Religion unhappily tends to lock onto "the law" and doctrine, onto dualism and judgmental thinking, the controlling axis of sin, guilt and punishment, and often onto the belief that its peculiar dogma makes it the sole and superior possessor of the Truth. The latter is particularly true of the Abrahamic traditions—Judaism, Islam, Christianity—which might explain the missionary compulsion of the latter to convert the whole world to its beliefs. This is a bit like arguing over which is the one "right" food at a Smorgasbord. Does potato salad hold a monopoly on Truth? Does white meat or red meat? Does chocolate have all the answers? Well, maybe, but you get my drift.

In the West particularly, religion seems less able, or willing, to address the needs of those probing the mysteries of the further journey. Although pockets of mystics thrive at its fringes, or in its closets, it feels at times that the flame of mysticism has been nearly extinguished. *God is spirit, and those who worship must worship in spirit and in truth*, Jesus taught (John 4:24). Perhaps the churches wrap themselves so tightly in their legalisms precisely because they can't handle the intimacy with God that the mystic welcomes with splayed heart. And so, many in the West have set out on individual spiritual quests, trying to rediscover the wisdom of ancient and Medieval Christianity, or gleaning what they can from Eastern and Middle-Eastern wisdom traditions who seem better and more experienced at this than their own churches.

We could suggest, cynically, that a direct conversation between God and the faithful would put the pastors, priests, mullahs, rabbis and other middlemen out of work. Mystics of all creeds have always been persecuted by the institutional church. The Jews killed the prophets and crucified Jesus. The Inquisition burned tens of thousands of sincere believers who merely wished to live in Biblical simplicity. Sufi poets had to write in code to protect their works from the pyre, and nine centuries after Jesus, the Muslim mystic al-Hallaj was crucified for saying that he and God were one—the same claim for which Jesus was labeled *blasphemer*.

The churches, it seems, prefer to focus on sin, to produce good citizens and regular donors. Like stern parents they warn us that God will love us *only* if we are obedient children and point out that, like Santa, he *knows* if we've been bad or good. It's all written down in the big book at heaven's gate. They teach us that God will respond to us—or not—based on our behavior, welcoming those who pray, smiting those who do not, or that God favors one people while excluding all others. God thus portrayed is a very small god indeed, with a heart not much bigger than the Grinch's before his conversion.

As a 9-year-old orphan I was bused across town with my mates each Sunday to a Church of the Nazarene. Stark black-and-white images of souls teetering between the sunrays of heaven and the flames of hell covered the walls, even in the children's Sunday school section. I still recoil decades later when I recall the day we were led to the front of the adult church. There we had to kneel and confess our sinfulness while elders hovered behind and over each of us, their fingernails digging into our shoulders. One-by-one my fellow orphans rose and left the church, but my elder was more obstinate (or perhaps thought I was). I could hear the engine of the school bus revving outside, ready to leave, but still he held me down until I finally wet my pants from sheer anxiety. Ah, that old-time religion—good enough for some, but not for me.

Once again we need to remind ourselves that *nothing we do can make God love us less; nothing we do can make God love us more*. Love is infinite and unconditional. Nor is it subject to change when we die. Love is independent of us. God is gracious, gentle, merciful, forgiving. We need not worry that the Father is itching to take us to the woodshed, in this life or the next. This may smack of heresy to those who use fear and guilt as control mechanisms to maintain order in the nation or the congregation, which also was largely the function of the Ten Commandments and much of the Old Testament, where God the Smiter made a regular appearance. Yet, centuries after the Torah was compiled, John the Apostle assured us that *God is Love* and even a saint like Teresa of Avila could view failings as learning opportunities. The holiest among us are imperfect, and without our flaws we wouldn't be a step lower than the angels, would we?

This business of law and sin are not the entire point here, however, nor whether we need specialists supervising our relationship with God. We can be in communion with God without the sacraments and other outward signs because true communion happens interiorly, and no authentic spiritual master has ever insisted that we need human intermediaries between God and us. Every mouthful we swallow is Eucharist when taken with thankful awareness of the divinity hiding within all creation.

> "I was six when I saw that everything was God, and my hair stood up, and all," Teddy said. "It was on a Sunday, I remember. My sister was a tiny child then, and she was drinking her milk, and all of a sudden I saw that she was God and the milk was God. I mean, all she was doing was pouring God into God, if you know what I mean."
> —J.D. Salinger, *Teddy*

In defense of religion, however, we can acknowledge that even the momentary glimpse of God's compassion offered by religion can have a lasting, future effect. Apart from the aspect of worship, those of us who attended church as youths received there our first inkling of something beyond. The mystics of every tradition were formed within the structures of formal religion and owe them that debt. All were introduced to mystery through the rituals and liturgy, sacred numbers, prayer, creeds and holy texts of the traditions into which they were born, though many outgrew their espaliers as they blossomed into wisdom. In the end, they didn't confuse the signs and symbols, the magical elements of religion, with ultimate Truth. Holy Church the Little, the precursor, prepares for Holy Church the Great in the same way that studious meditation on sacred scriptures (gaining knowledge of God) and self-examination (gaining knowledge of ourselves) prepare us for the thought-less prayer of contemplation and the infusion of Love. For those at a preliminary stage of the journey or still vested in the surface of life, formal religion can be a tremendous resource. It's always been a good place to start, comparable to the stage of initiates in the ancient mystery schools. We must dig beneath the surface of religion, however, to reach the levels of the adepts and masters.

> God has the same relationship to institutional religion as wellness has to organized medicine. Neither God nor wellness can be confined to either establishment, but religious traditions and medical practices contain wise and vital resources that can aid wellness or deepen spirituality.
> —Robert Morris

Religious institutions also offer their members a sense of community, although this often tends to the social rather than the spiritual. Still, stretching one's social muscles can be useful insofar as interaction takes us out of ourselves. Rubbing against others in all kinds of settings is one of the primary ways we grow. And to the extent that we can pierce through the external practices and trappings of a church community, we can touch its sacred core.

We also can allow the contributions of these magnificent organizations to art and the economy with their beautiful houses of worship, music, paintings, sculptures and stained-glass windows, as well as their contributions to philosophy, theology and religious *reasoning* in general. Holy Church the Little has borne many a pilgrim to the furthest frontiers the rational mind can explore. But those who seek full enlightenment, both in the West and in the East, eventually feel the need to break through all systems based on "isms," whether they are cultural, social, political or religious. Even those of us who continue a formal religious practice need to stay focused on the Spirit behind our specific *ism*, to see the singular Truth burning at its heart.

> The work of the Church in the world is not to teach the mysteries of life, so much as to persuade the soul to that

arduous degree of purity at which God himself becomes her teacher. The work of the Church ends when the knowledge of God begins.[11]

To my mind, the real difficulty with official religion for the traveler on the mystic way is that it reinforces the notion of separation between God and us, and in this respect actually hinders spiritual progress. The formal prayers of religion, for example, invariably are directed to a transcendent deity, a being *out* there or *up* there, the God of similes, the avatar who came to earth but then left again and now dwells in a heaven infinitely removed from our imperfect world. Belief in our separation from the Godhead, as I keep insisting, is the fundamental dualism that proves fatal to enlightenment. Once we've had a peek through this latticework, however, we can empathize with Martin Buber who once sighed: *it pains me to speak of God in the third person*. Yet this is the everyday language of formal religion.

The question arises, then, where can we begin our search for the indwelling God, for our true Self, beyond the houses of worship? Where can we find the immanent and omnipresent God who will lead us home to Source? We can find one answer in the nature mysticism of Celtic spirituality and the Eastern religious traditions or the musings of a Henry David Thoreau. Francis of Assisi was a son of the institutional church. He sought papal approval of his new order to avoid the heretic label and the stake, the fate of many of his contemporaries who espoused radical poverty. At heart, however, he was a profound nature mystic, as his "Canticle of the Sun" attests. His approach to the Deity would encourage us to begin our search for God in visible creation—to seek the *face of God* according to the psalmist, or in the East, to become conscious of the *body of the Buddha* in its manifold expressions in the universe.

Instruction lies all around us and as we delve into it, as we let the cosmos teach us the natural flow of our lives, we discover the creator in all that is, including us—the hidden radiance, the divine spark, waiting to be released from its

---

[11] Coventry Patmore, *The Rod, the Root, and the Flower,* 2nd Edition, (London: Covent Garden, 1907)

natural shells. We cannot separate God and the universe. As Thomas Aquinas explained, *a mistake about creation is a mistake about God*. Over time this so-called *positive way*, this giant step toward oneness, expands our grasp of our unity with the rest of existence, of brotherhood and sisterhood with all else that is.

Chapter 2. The Positive Way

Seeking God's Face

> He who knew nothing other than creatures would have no need for thinking or sermons, for each creature is full of God.
> —Meister Eckhart

> Nature is the *Great Mysterious*,
> the *religion before religion*.
> —Peter Matthiessen

In our first days on the mystic way we meander through familiar scenes, led toward the God of images we remember from childhood, God fully clothed, dressed up like a doll or the divine infant of Prague. Among these myriad representations is God the Creator, the God who decreed, *let there be light,* back when all things came to be. For this God, the universe is the ongoing manifestation of his creative power, his *becoming*, and the living shrine in which he dwells among us.

The route to the Being we perceive through the visible universe is called the *positive way*. Later, we will probe in darkness and denial the *negative way*, the way of self-naughting, of reduction to utter no-thing, in search of the ineffable Godhead behind all imagining and all perception. For the record, in spiritual writings these two paths are also referred to as the *via positiva* toward the *cataphatic God* and the *via negativa* toward the *apophatic God*.

> The soul can only be pure and white like snow if you make a void in yourself—or, on the contrary, if you lose yourself in the totality of creation.
> —Ananda Moyi

Those familiar with the Hasidic tradition might see in these seemingly opposed approaches the teachings of the Baal Shem Tov, who believed the Divine accommodates Itself to our level of understanding through the visible world, and the negative proclamations of the tormented Reb Menahem Mendl of Kotzk (the Kotzker), but both paths lead to the same destination. Let's look first at the positive route on which we *lose* ourselves *in the totality of creation.*

Amongst many other divine images, that of the Father is particularly beloved. When Jesus taught his followers the Lord's Prayer, his opening word, the word we translate as *Father*, was in the Aramaic, *Abwoon*—the Father as *author of the universe.* The sound *Abwoon*, according to Neil Douglas-Klotz,[12] consists of four parts:

A: The Absolute, only Being, pure Oneness and Unity;

bw: a birthing, a creation, as if from the *interior* of this Oneness;

oo: the breath or spirit that carries this flow, linked to the Aramaic phrase *rukha d'qoodsha*, later translated as *Holy Spirit*;

n: the vibration of this creative breath from Oneness at it touches and interpenetrates form, including us.

Thus *Abwoon*, or *Father*, can be interpreted as *That which manifests uniquely through all existence, the breath that finds Its anchor in creation.* Just as words flow forth, yet remain in the mind of the speaker, the creative breath of God flows from its origin yet ever remains within the divine Mind.

Our immediate reaction when we ponder the universe, even here at the base of Mystic Mountain, is humbling wonder bordering on awe. Divinity surrounds and envelops us, brimming up and shining through our ordinary awareness in all that is, from the furthest galaxy to the smallest subatomic particle. While we may be puzzled by the creator's inordinate fondness for bugs and suns, we are nonetheless stirred by the immense miracle, the marvel of it all, and a vision of the One that contains in Its Being all the diversity of the visible and imaginable universe. In her poem "Messenger," Mary Oliver sees her *work* as standing still, learning reverence from such astonishments as a phoebe, blue plums or a clam buried deep

---

[12] Neil Douglas-Klotz (translator), *Prayers of the Cosmos: Meditations on the Aramaic Words of Jesus* (New York: HarperCollins, 1994). Cited in John Sack, *Yearning for the Father: The Lord's Prayer and the Mystic Journey*, (Prescott: Hohm Press, 2006), pp. 37-39.

in speckled sand—all those divine marvels opened to us through our senses, even as their deeper truth opens to our minds and souls. Although they are part of the physical universe, in such moments they extend beyond time and space in the same way that *becoming* shades into *being*. When we soften our gaze as we look out at nature, we can see the energetic aura surrounding each shrub and the face emerging from every tree, the face of God disclosing Itself to the receptive observer. We stand *always* on holy ground, although we seldom see it.

Gerard Manley Hopkins coined a term for this vision: *inscape*. For him, as it must be for us, the word was a verb, to escape inward, as well as a noun, our inner landscape, nature itself turned inward. Creation, he felt, *should after its manner give God being in return for the being He has given it*. Nature *is word, expression, news of God. Its purpose, its purport, its meaning, is God, and its life or work [is] to name and praise Him.*

> I had been sitting in the garden working and had just finished. ... It was still and peaceful—around me and within me. ... Then it began to come, that infinite tenderness, which is purer and deeper than that of lovers, or of a father toward his child. It was in me, but it also came to me, as the air came to my lungs. ... I inhaled the tenderness.
>
> The deep tenderness ... extended further and further—it became all present. ... This was my first actual meeting with Reality; ... a *Now that is* and a *Now that happens*. ... Time and space, characteristics of the *Now that happens*, were, so to speak, "outside." ... It is the continuously active creation with all its birth throes. I saw time and space as instruments of this creation. They come into existence with it and in the course of it, and with it they come to an end. The Newly Created stands in the *Now [that is]* and discards these tools. The freedom, the real *Being* begins.[13]

---

[13] Johannes Anker-Larsen, *With the Door Open* (London and New York: Macmillan, 1931)

Pondering creation can reduce our egos to disturbingly small proportions. For example, a cubic foot of soil contains more living organisms than the number of people living here in the United States. Earth is very much a living system. Quite possibly, the Biblical version of creation, which said that God formed everything on earth—every plant, every animal and every bit of terrain—to serve humankind, has given us an inflated sense of our importance. Who is to say that trees were not created or did not evolve primarily to offer food and shelter to birds, monkeys, sloths and squirrels, albeit some also give us fruit and lumber and heat? Only recently in our history have we ventured into jungles that for many millennia were the exclusive province of the wild things. Night, likewise, belonged to the prowlers of the dark with their enhanced nocturnal vision, while humankind kept the bonfire burning and cowered in its caves and huts. And do the seas not provide for the creatures that swim and scuttle there above all others? We, that is, our infinitesimal human selves, make up but a tiny portion of the landscape, even on this one slight planet, and are barely conceivable in the immense backdrop of the universe.

And yet we are *immense* in our spiritual connection to Divinity. Perhaps the greatest wonder in creation is the recognition that if the Godhead manifests through the entire cosmos, then It must manifest through us as well, through our limbs and our minds, through each cell in our bodies, through our souls and our spirits—that our next heartbeat, in fact, derives from this generous Source. Spirit shines forth as the immediacy of all being. An awakening to the Divinity of which we are an expression begins to stir within us. We learn to expand beyond personal consciousness, and open ourselves to the point where we contain all things in God. We begin to understand how Love permeates the inmost dimension of our spirits and how it is from this sanctuary common to each of us that It continuously performs Its act of *becoming* through creation, working through us as helpers and co-creators.

But Divinity also *envelops* us. Like joyful porpoises, we cavort in a sacred sea, an ocean of boundless affection, whose waters enfold and wash through us. We are in Spirit and Spirit is in us, as Paul explained to the Council of the Areopagus in

Athens: *Indeed he is not far from any of us, since it is in him that we live and move and have our being* (Acts 17:28). Kabir likened the soul to a pitcher filled with water which is simultaneously submerged in a great pool of water. Water within, water without!

> The day of my spiritual awakening was the day I saw, and knew that I saw, God in all things and all things in God.
> —Mechtild of Magdeburg

Our study of nature also exposes its grim side, of course, such as the anything-but-symbiotic pairings of predator and prey, the devastation of natural disasters, Mother Nature's callousness or indifference towards our personal ambitions, and enough cruelty to make us question the benevolence of the Creator—what might be called the negative aspect of the positive way. Side-by-side with the preservers of creation in the Hindu and Greek pantheons are the angry destroyer gods, the face of God we often see scowling through the early books of the Judeo-Christian Bible.

We can't comprehend or justify this, for we'd like to think we would have come up with a gentler universe had it been left to us. We can complain to the Creator about Its inscrutability, but the only answer we are likely to receive is, *the heavens are as high above earth as my ways are above your ways, my thoughts above your thoughts* (Isaiah 55:9). We are baffled at the way the Godhead enfolds both pain and joy within the totality of Its being. Suffice it to say, only when the larger scheme of cosmic evolution is revealed to us will we begin to appreciate the divine intent. Meanwhile, these observations train and equip us to deal with unexpected surprises, with suffering and disappointment, which in nature coexist with breathtaking splendor and amazement.

Humans, philosophers and theologians in particular, have for centuries scratched their collective head over the *how* of divine existence within us, within scrub brush, scrub jays and scrub oaks, within "empty" space and Higgs bosons or whatever membrane glues the universe together. Are we talking *pantheism* (that tree is God) or *panentheism* (God interpenetrates the tree, but eternally extends beyond it. God's essence is Being, Its manifestation always Becoming.)?

Part of the Jewish belief is that the divine life-force must be present for creation to hold together. *There is nothing that does not contain a glint of holiness, for without it nothing could possibly exist.* Should God retract this life-force from the universe for even a moment, nature, including human nature, would revert to its pre-creation state, to nothingness.

> You hide your face, they are dismayed;
> you take back your spirit, they die,
> returning to the dust from which they came.
> You send forth your spirit, they are created;
> And you renew the face of the earth.
> —Psalm 104

In this sense we can say we already exist in a state of union with Divinity, long before we are aware of this union. If we were not continually present within the divine awareness, we would cease to be. This was also the revelation that came to Julian of Norwich: *and again God spoke to me, "It [creation] lasts, both now and forever, because I cherish it." And I understood that everything has its being owing to God's care and love.* Clearly there is limitless affection sustaining the universe, reminding us with each pulsing of the blood through our veins of God's love for us and the totality of creation.

Judaism also holds that God is an absolute unity, and that It is perfectly simple. If God's sustaining power is within nature, then the divine *essence* is also within nature. God's presence, or *Shekhinah*, indwells the world. A Buddhist might say that, moment after moment, everything emerges from nothingness and that whether we live in delusion or become one with our surroundings depends on our acceptance of what is. Emptiness is emptiness and form is form. Some Hindus or new-age devotees, on the other hand, would dismiss all of these theories, proclaiming that all we see—including our individual forms—is illusory, and that nothing exists *but* God. This is not necessarily in accord with Hindu scripture, however.

> The God who is in the fire,
> the God who is in the water,
> the God who has entered into the world,

> the God who is in the plants and the trees,
> adoration to that God, adoration to him.
> —*Svetasvatara Upanishad*, 2:17

As with the troupe of angels dancing on the head of a pin, the theorizing and debate about the *how* of God's presence is less important than waking to the *now* of that mystery, recognizing the divine presence as It plays out in our lives, within us and around us, in the very split-second you are reading this. That power is *somehow* hidden at the core of creation and that is enough. Recognizing this sacred omnipresence is a major milestone on the path to union.

> God lets us experience his presence even now in all that surrounds us. Imagine how it must be when we can see him face-to-face!"
> —Trappist Brother Elias

Alas, we do not see God face-to-face here on earth and may feel frustrated that we cannot reciprocate the generosity of a nonvisible Being. But as our love for that Being blazes more strongly within us, we realize that we *can* show love by caring for Its myriad, visible manifestations. When I set out water on hot summer days for the deer and birds that visit our yard, I am loving the Godhead through Its creatures. When I prune and fertilize the fruit trees in our pocket orchard, I'm returning some small measure of God's love for me. Preserving and fostering the environment not only leaves a legacy for future generations, but is a way to say *I love you* to the Being who shines through earth's limitless variety. When I bring coffee to my dear wife in the morning, or share sexual joy with her in the night, I am through my actions expressing my love for God, for she too manifests the Divine. When I feed or exercise my own body or nurture my mind and spirit, I am loving God—in addition to giving thanks for this gift of life. In fact, Bernard of Clairvaux called this the highest rung on the ladder of love, when we come to love ourselves for God's sake.

The Near and Far God

Contemplating nature, the display of God's "face," going on retreats and pilgrimages, self-improvement workshops, fidelity to prayer and other spiritual practices—all work to deepen and purify awareness of divine presence in our lives. During these halting, early steps up the mountain, God enters our spirits through numerous portals and wanders quietly about, a mysterious visitor who makes us wish to know more *about* It, while at the same time making us want to *be* like It. We also are growing in self-awareness, gradually conceding the impermanence of the small self who inhabits this temporal body. We sense an increase in gratitude towards this Being who has borne with us for all these decades while we've bumbled about, trying with mixed success to figure out the purpose of life. We briefly catch sight as well of our higher, eternal Self at work, the Self that communicates with the Love indwelling and ordering all creation.

Initially, we are drawn to images of God presented to us in youth, then move on to conceptions of that Being as It touches us through the observable universe. Our feeling for this *near* God is deepening.

But something within us resists the urge to linger at the traces of infinity in the visible world, the footprints showing where God has passed, for our intuition (that inner whispering of Spirit) tells us there is something surpassing even these recent sightings. We can glimpse Love in nature and try to imagine how It resides within us, but It still enjoys Its game of hide-and-seek, darting in-and-out of the shadows of our minds. Thus, while mulling the impact of divine immanence and omnipresence in our temporal, spatial world, we also experience a growing urge to discover the Transcendence that *eternally Is*—outside of time and place, outside of thought and imagination, predating creation—the Ein Sof that *exists* before It had names like Elohim or Yahweh or El Shaddai, the Ekam Sat behind the trimurti of Brahma, Vishnu and Shiva, the Godhead behind the trinity of Father, Son and Holy Spirit, the One behind all distinctions, all separation—in short, *That-Which-Is*.

The stakes have been raised in our pursuit of mystery even though we still must concede with the Bengali poet Tagore,

> The song I came to sing
> remains unsung to this day.
> I have spent my days stringing

> and unstringing my instrument. ...
> I have not ... listened to his voice;
> only I have heard his gentle footsteps
> from the road before my house. ...
> But the lamp has not been lit
> and I cannot ask him into my house;
> I live in the hope of meeting with him;
> but this meeting is not yet.
> —Rabindranath Tagore

Our search has just begun, of course. We have not yet felt the desperate longing of the betrothed in the Song of Songs who wanders the city by night in search of her Beloved. Someday, but not yet, we too will be asked to search our inner terrain for the *far* God in the darkness of unknowing, with the lantern of reason snuffed. The journey will get murkier and at times the path will vanish altogether in trackless badlands. But not yet.

The betrothed describes, further, how the night watchmen wounded and stripped her (Song of Songs, 5:6-7) and this stripping too is part of the quest. Wounds of love and utter nakedness define the state in which we will one day be left, bereft, after passing through the purifying nights of the senses and spirit.

For now, though, we continue to live in *ordinary mind*. Despite our best intentions, we still see God as other than ourselves. To take the next step, we need the inpouring of Grace that allows words about God to penetrate our hearts as well as our minds. We need to *live* God's immediate presence, not just grasp "God here-and-now" as a mental concept.

After this our initiation in faithful practice and detachment, we find ourselves turning ever more towards the silence within while the exterior world fades to irrelevance. Wordless prayer and contemplation begin to displace discursive meditation, and Love takes on a growing role in our transformation. Nature becomes increasingly transparent, the veil between creature and Creator thinner. Glimpses of Divinity become a steady gaze.

Understandably, we want to leap forward and share the delight of those experiencing higher states of contemplation, to run while we are still learning to toddle, to eat solid food before we have been weaned, but we need to remind ourselves that all advance is subject to God's timing. We can hope, though, that as we near the crossover from the active to the passive stage of the way, however many years it takes to reach that place, we will be ready to receive the gift of breakthrough into the next level of awareness.

Every breakthrough to a higher level, we quickly learn, demands that we give up more of our small self, that we let go and let go until finally nothing of *us* is left to surrender. This is the price to be paid for each expansion of our awareness. Less and less in control of our pilgrimage, we must trust Love to guide us in deepening darkness down an undefined trail. Know that these are sacred haunts, however, rich in unforeseeable surprises designed to adorn our spirits until we finally are ready to be presented to the Beloved.

God and I are One

When we began the active, preparation phase of the journey, we had to attack the thickets of Mystic Mountain's lowest slopes. And while we still have much work to do on our own and need to maintain our focus, we now wait in expectation for Love to complete this groundwork and to further purify us.

The first phase of the pilgrimage, however, is half over. We have nearly cleared the tangle of underbrush and the towering distraction of surrounding trees. Even though we are still at a relatively early juncture, we may suddenly find ourselves in an instantaneous flash welcomed into the next level of awareness. This jump is nothing short of electrifying, like the image that captures the movement:

> When peaceful silence lay over all
> and night had run the half of her swift course,
> down from the heavens, from the royal throne,
> leapt your all-powerful Word.
> —Wisdom 18:14-15

What is the function of this Word or, for that matter, the function of true words in general? Do they not reveal what has been hidden or is not yet understood? In this case, the role of the Word is to expose the Godhead to us and not only to expose It, but to make It *real* and *substantial*, within us.

This revelation conveys the *certainty* that we are One with the Godhead. We have come across the concept by now in our spiritual reading, but in this instant we *experience* the immediacy of this Oneness both consciously and subliminally as a pure gift of Love, feel its actuality in our hearts. It is a *happening* that transcends body and mind, argument or reason, transporting us infinitely beyond the knowing of our senses, beyond the tantalizing, *intellectual* comprehension of Oneness, allowing us to intuit in some secret vein the truth the words illustrate.

Meister Eckhart used the term "breakthrough" (*durchbruch*) to describe this experience. *In this breakthrough I discover that God and I are one*, he said, and the "God" he referred to is That-Which-Is, the Godhead concealed behind all human images and imagination. People create mental likenesses of God for their own sake; God certainly doesn't need them. For this reason Meister Eckhart prayed elsewhere, *God, rid me of god*, begging that he might sink not merely into the Creator, but more deeply into That which lies eternally behind creation, behind every creaturely notion of God. *His unconditioned Being is above god and all distinctions*, Eckhart preached.

> When I flowed out from God, all things spoke, god is. But this cannot make me happy, because it makes me understand that I am a creature. In [this] breakthrough, on the other hand, where I stand free of my own will and of the will of god and of all his works and of god himself, there I am above all creatures and am neither god nor creature. Rather I am what I once was and what I shall remain now and forever. ... For in this breakthrough I discover that God and I are one.[14]

---

[14]Meister Eckhart, Sermon *Beati Pauperes Spiritu* ("Blessed are the poor in spirit ..."). In these and other quotations from Meister Eckhart, "God" refers to That-Which-Is; "god" refers to Divinity as filtered through human imagination.

Elsewhere, in a Christmas sermon based on the words from the Book of Wisdom quoted above, Meister Eckhart compares this awakening to Oneness in the Godhead to a lightning flash that (quoting Augustine) *radiates and sparkles before my soul.* He also cites a "pagan master" who says of this sparkling, *If I could grasp it, I would know all Truth.* The purpose of this burst of light, this illumination, is that we should *yearn and sigh after it*, like children chasing fireflies through the twilight of a summer evening. In the midst of our spiritual efforts, we are afforded this rare preview of the profundity to which we are joined, enough of a foretaste that it whets our longing for the limitless and reorders our priorities forever. In this instant, our hearts open fully wide, embracing the Divine, for we have sampled That without which life can never again feel complete. It is just enough and just as it should be, for as an Irish poet wrote, *through a chink too wide comes no wonder*, and on the positive way we have been traveling, astonishment is the arm-in-arm companion of awe. In my own work I've discovered that a mite of muddle in the mind sometimes uncovers wonders unsuspected when writing wide-awake.

The difference between this breakthrough and union at the highest level is that our small self still intrudes itself into the process. Apart from the *experience* of Oneness, *something* still thinks "God and I are one." The mind also may wonder: *how can I stay forever in this marvelous place?* Even as we experience lovely, almost beatific, union with Pure Being, something within us is agreeing, *it's true, I AM That.* The part agreeing is ego, however, not pure "Is-Ness," and thus a subtle separation remains. Be aware always that the self, in its frenzy for self-preservation, will most willingly and eagerly betray our best chance for happiness, struggling to keep us imprisoned in our false and foolish frames of mind. It will lose this particular battle, however. Yes, there is this subtle foray on ego's part, but our awareness nevertheless has been unalterably refined by this revelation.

The breakthrough, however deeply we take it in, marks a critical milepost on the inner pathway of every sincere seeker, the point of no return, for from this moment, we know there is no going back, nor even looking back, to the world we left behind. The path has vanished behind us.

In this moment, all we know is that we have caught sight of That-Which-Is beyond the mind, beyond the soul, beyond all that constitutes our small self. We know too that the effect of this sighting will last forever. Even deeper than the *spark* at the center of our spirit is something so *like* the Godhead that it already is one with Divinity and feels *no need* to merge with It, a profundity that we will fully understand only in the final breakthrough, at death. This experience also confirms that we have lost control of our pilgrimage, that from this point we will be led by a force beyond our knowing or understanding or resisting. The insight is reassuring beyond measure.

In the silence at the center of our being where no image can penetrate, we have touched primordial Silence, the Stillness that infinitely *is*, before creation. We know now that we partake of the Nameless behind every human description of god, the Mysterious behind all mystery, the Eternal behind all time. We have entered That-Which-Is by experiencing It and in this moment, by *becoming* It. The Godhead is no longer theoretical. *It* actually is, and exists as the highest consciousness, the true Self, of each of us (or in Buddhist terms, as no-self). This realization takes one's breath away each time it rises to the level of awareness.

The breakthrough represents a cosmic leap—particularly for those of us raised in the West—and Eckhart ended this sermon by reassuring his listeners: *If anyone cannot understand this discourse, let them not trouble their hearts about it. For as long as people do not equal this truth, they will not understand my speech, for it is an unveiled truth that has come immediately from the heart of God.* Certainly, the inquisitors of his day didn't grasp it. They condemned his sublime works and assuredly would have burned him with them had he not died before the conclusion of his trial.

This close encounter with Ultimate Being is literally *mind-blowing*; it outstrips anything the rational mind or the imagination in its maddest fancies could possibly conjure. We have *experienced* union with That-Which-Is in the inmost region of our spirit, in a depth within us that cannot be plumbed by reason or metaphors. We still cannot guess Its form, for the Word's leap occurs at night, yet we now understand that we do, *really do*, share in Divinity, having been invited to do so from all eternity!

We were created by love, for love, and so that we should love. *Before I formed you in the womb, I knew you.* (Jeremiah 1:5) These are words that apply to each of us. We were planned for from all eternity. None of us is a mere divine afterthought. None of us is an accident. *Before the foundation of the world* (John 17:24), God chose us to be his children.[15]

When Meister Eckhart exclaimed, *God and I are One*, he of course referred to the Godhead that exists beyond creation, the Being in which there is neither man nor nature. As for the *I* that shares this Oneness, he did not mean his small self—not the man labeled *Eckhart*, not the one who preached marvelous sermons, wandered Europe and finally died conversing with a tree. That *I* is not *It*. As he explained in the earlier quotation, it is the *I* outside human will or human interpretation of God's will. This *I* stands outside creation, before it entered time and space, outside any thought of God.

He taught that we are, every one of us, that *All* as It *is* before time came to be. *It* ones Itself with the spirit within each of us that will outlive our temporality, that higher Self that Joseph Campbell called, *the footprint of the All, for by it one knows the All—just as, verily, by following a footprint one finds cattle that have been lost.* The Japanese ox-herding parables convey the same message. Follow the ox prints to the source of enlightenment. If we focus on and follow our higher Self, it will lead us home, where we will rediscover, among other marvels, that we have ever been wholly lovable and loving.

God does not suddenly arrive within us or envelop us, of course, nor are we suddenly subsumed into the Godhead. This union has eternally been. What has changed is our *awareness* of God's constant presence and how we partake in It, the *fact* that in God we do have our being. Oneness is no longer a mere

---

[15] Desmond Tutu, Introduction to *An African Prayer Book* (New York: Doubleday, 1995)

concept, a fanciful notion we want to hold in our hearts, but has become a personal conviction, a certainty, and an assurance of our link to Divinity. Before this breakthrough, we relate to God as other than ourselves; after the breakthrough, we feel our equivalence. Like Francis of Assisi, who prayed constantly, *my God and my all*, we are led to the clear realization: *there is nothing here, there is no one here, but God*. Given this awareness, Francis could surface from his dim cave into the sunshine of Monte Subasio and see God in whatever direction he looked—gazing back at him from the eyes of each person he met, from every aspect of creation, from Brother Sun and Sister Moon. This is why he could welcome joyfully his Sister Bodily Death.

While this revelation is startling to us in the West, it is common fare in the Eastern wisdom traditions. It is *Identity* in Islam, the gateway to *satori* in Zen Buddhism and *nirvana*, union with the Brahman, in Hinduism. And while seekers in the East may be as slow as we to waken to this wonder, the belief in creation's Oneness with the Ground of Being is the basic bread of Oriental religions. Christianity teaches us that Jesus was both God and man; in the East, everyone is viewed as truly God as well as truly human. *Tat tvam asi—You are It*—Aruni tells his son Svetaketu in the Chandogya Upanishad, some 800 years before the Christ of the West appeared on earth. We are not, nor have ever been, exiles divorced from Divinity, deported from "heaven" the way Adam and Eve were cast out from the garden. The breakthrough experience assures us That-Which-Is dwells within each of us, as us, and only waits to be rediscovered at ever deeper levels as we continue the journey inward. The true Self affirms, in the spirit of Aruni: *I* am already That. I *am* already That. I am *already* That. I am already *That*.

Heirs of God through adoption

Western, Middle Eastern, or Hindu communities are likely not as comfortable with the concept of Godhead as Void or No-Thing-Ness or Is-Ness as a Buddhist might be. We are used to thinking of God as a divine *person* to whom we can relate individually, the Entity who walked through paradise with the first humans, spoke directly to the patriarchs and prophets and, like Jesus and Krishna, has visited the earth many times in human form. This personification is normal, particularly at the outset of our pilgrimage. The Jewish and Christian scriptures tell us that we were created in the image and likeness of God and meant to share in the divine nature. Jesus, whether he was born a fully-enlightened, divine avatar, or matured into this level of consciousness in the course of his own journey, clearly recognized his identity with—and lived totally in harmony with—Ultimate Being. He envisioned this identity as a relationship between a loving, but demanding, Father and himself, the obedient Son. *Not my will but thine be done*, he groaned in the garden of Gethsemane, even though he knew that very night the Father's will would require his life.

Constantly aware of his unity with the Father, he wished the same for his followers: *May they all be one, just as, Father, you are in me and I am in you, so that they also may be one in us* (John 17:21). This Father is not solely *Abwoon*, the Source of all creation, but also *Abba*—a word derived from the same root as *Abwoon* and the most intimate name possible to describe the father-child connection, much like our word *Papa*. Paul used this term in his letters to the Romans and Galatians, and so it has become the fundamental vision of the Christian to awaken to this relationship in the depths of his or her spirit. We are children of the Father and as such share in the inheritance of the Son, which is nothing less than eternal bliss in the kingdom of heaven:

> You received the Spirit of adoption, enabling us to cry out, "*Abba*, Father." The Spirit himself joins with our spirit to bear witness that we are children of God, and if we are children, then we are heirs, heirs of God and joint-heirs with Christ.
>
> —Romans 8:15-17

Recognizing the full impact of co-inheritance is a wonderful aspect of this breakthrough. As joint heirs of the Father with the Christ, we share in Its divinity, in Christ-consciousness, and furthermore can receive and enjoy our inheritance *now*, while we still inhabit earth. The kingdom of heaven is here among us. Teresa of Avila could barely get past the opening word of the Lord's Prayer (*Padre* or *Pater* in her case) once she grasped the full impact of this revelation, that she and her nuns were in truth daughters of the loving Father (*Way of Perfection*, 27:1-2).

Some side-effects of breakthrough

A witness to Eckhart's death said it seemed he was *creating* the tree to which he was speaking before he collapsed. Through adoption, you see, we become co-creators of the universe alongside God's Word. With this realization, however, comes the more subtle recognition that we would not move mountains, no matter how great our faith, because we would remember why we set them there in the first place. Yet, "miraculous" acts that defy the laws of physics or nature are not extraordinary to those immersed in this awareness. After the breakthrough, we are miracle-ready. We can exhale the creative breath along with Spirit, whose likeness we are, even in the seemingly trivial, minute-to-minute events of our human lives. Lama Govinda noted truly that *the forces that move the cosmos are no different from those that move the human soul*. Dylan Thomas wrote of the force that drives the green shoot to flower and claimed with equal assurance that it was the same force that drove him.

A small example: as a skinny Trappist novice in Kentucky in my late teens, I was asked to thin aspen saplings in the monastery's woodlands. I worked alone and when the upper branches of one tree entangled with its neighbors, I couldn't bring it down, could only swing it back and forth, although I'd completely axed away its base. Praying for help while my hands still gripped the tree's trunk, I felt a rush like an electric current flow from my shoulders and down the length my arms. When the current reached my hands, the tree flew away as easily and cleanly as a limb tossed onto a slash pile.

A later incident during a particularly threatening windstorm startled me to the core, besides leaving me feeling somewhat sheepish. I lived at that time in the Santa Cruz Mountains of California, in a cabin surrounded by soaring Douglas Firs. A nasty squall with deafening gusts had kept me awake and fearful all night because the shallow-rooted trees were known to topple and crush houses in the area. I had by then been exposed to the notion of oneness with God during a stint in India, and about three o'clock in the morning decided to put it to the test. *If I am That, certainly I can calm a storm*, I thought and in my middle-of-the-night hypnogogic jumble yelled aloud, "Shut up!" *Immediately*, the forest outside my home became utterly silent and naught so much as a zephyr disturbed my sleep the rest of the night. Yow!

A woman friend worked alone in her garden one evening, trying to reposition a boulder by rolling it up a short incline and onto a berm. She couldn't budge it, but related later how, after a moment of centering within, she again tried to move the rock, which practically rolled itself up the rise and fell into the exact position she wanted.

I should note in these instances that these co-creative, so-called *miracles* are not mystical acts in the highest sense. The woman and I were still exercising our individual wills, wanting to achieve specific results. The same might be said of the many cases of healing prayer that could be cited here. Such prayer is acquisitive, but as we shall see later, the final stripping of the human spirit demands total surrender of the will, of all such personal desires on our part so Love can work untrammeled through us.

Unmitigated *joy*, pervasive bliss, is another effect of glimpsing our true Self. No ordinary experience compares to this sudden awareness of our unity with That-Which-Is and we automatically grin when we reflect on it, or on the Godhead immanent within us. Initially this bliss may be fleeting, like the revelation that inspired it, lasting only as long as the ecstatic moment, but as we advance, quiet joy becomes our abiding disposition. Gradually, everything that happens to us, every task we take on, no matter how burdensome it *should* feel, becomes a source of happiness. *God comes to you disguised as your life*, Paula D'Arcy once observed. The yoke may seem heavy during our efforts at detachment, but in this next phase becomes sweet and light.

My wife and I made a pilgrimage to Italy, to the hill country surrounding Assisi. En route, we stopped in Rome, visited St. Peter's Basilica, and while there slipped through the curtain separating the adoration chapel from the main cathedral and its milling tourists. This chapel is an extremely solemn setting for Roman Catholics, as the Eucharist, believed to be Jesus himself, is displayed on its altar. As soon as we entered, however, I broke into a wide smile and had to fight an urge to dance down the aisle. Finally, I left the chapel for fear of disrupting the somber worship of those kneeling around us. As I explained to my puzzled wife later, *the Father within me kept leaping for joy to see his Son on the altar and I could scarcely contain him.* Not so quiet joy!

Another effect of this breakthrough and the experience of Ultimate Being at our center is the realization that our temporal, physical selves are sanctuaries housing the holy of holies—no less so than the world's most magnificent cathedrals and temples. In Psalm 27 the cantor chants,

> There is one thing I ask of the Lord, for this I long, to dwell in the house of the lord all the days of my life, to savor the sweetness of the Lord, to behold his temple.

Now we realize we *are* that temple, not just as individuals, but as a mystical collective, which cannot but affect our perception of our fellow beings.

When we experience this breakthrough, when we *know* in a blaze of certainty that *God and I are One*, we also gain some inkling of the vastness of the human spirit, of our limitless expanse that can encompass the whole universe and reach out to touch the Godhead beyond the cosmos. On the ceiling of the Sistine Chapel, God touches Adam's fingertip, but after this revelation, we can reach out to It as well. It is natural when sitting in contemplation for the eyes to roll upward, taking in the night or daytime sky as the soul expands. Perhaps this is why so many paintings of saints depict them with their eyes lifted toward the sun or stars.

Blissful as we may feel, however, we also recognize that even though our spirit is fully engaged with God, *our small self still has work to do*, is still caught up in decidedly nonspiritual realms. That danged humanity again! While the breakthrough into God is continuously happening within us, we can normally perceive it only insofar as we are *silent*, that is, free of all imagery and any residue from the mindset of illusion. At the same time, our *small self*-awareness remains disturbingly obvious. We find ourselves literally led back to earth, to our day-to-day business on the planet. But we now know, at least, that the greatest miracle that could occur in our lives would be the complete and permanent transfiguration of our being—body, mind, soul and spirit. It is happening, but John of the Cross calls all transformation short of our final crossing but a *sketch of Love*.

> At this period the soul feels that she is rushing toward God as rapidly as a falling stone when nearing its center. ... She knows, too, that she is like a sketch or the first draft of a drawing and calls out to the one who did this sketch to finish the painting.[16]

This call to the Artist is significant, for although we still have much more to do on our own, we are nearing that crossing where change becomes more the provenance of Love than the effort of the individual, where Spirit completes the sketch.

After the Breakthrough

> Now, let your will be your guide.
> You're past the steep and past the narrow paths.
> —Dante, *Purgatorio*, Canto 27

Virgil spoke these comforting words to Dante as they were about to enter the earthly paradise, the antechamber to the celestial paradise that lay ahead. He meant in effect, *I've brought you as far as intellect can and from here a superior being must direct you*. On the mystic way, we likewise are about to enter an earthly paradise even as we approach the limits of the rational mind. The experience of our shared divinity, combined with our proven commitment to rid ourselves of all that is not God, works to free us finally from the thickets tangling the lower slope of Mystic Mountain. Our inner landscape opens upon a new vista. The path through the wood widens, entanglements are sparse, and we can see what appears to be a large clearing just up the trail.

One aspect of the joy we experience at this time comes from a sense that the hardest part of the journey, the effort we put into purging and purifying our senses and intellects and

---

[16] John of the Cross, *Spiritual Canticle*, 12.1

the sensual part of the soul, will soon be over—or be taken over by the inpouring of Love. We can for a time enjoy a respite before we encounter the subtler aspects of purgation, a moment to delight in God's bounty and love as we have come to know it. In traditional mystical terms, we are entering the phase of illumination.

The area just above the tree line is a pleasant meadow of tall grass and wildflowers, the sort of place hikers might rest for lunch before continuing higher up the mountain. Up the path we will enter the arid high desert, largely hidden at its uppermost slopes in the cloud of unknowing, where Love will complete the annihilation of the ego, but for now, this time of consolation in the meadow is most welcome.

The recent breakthrough was our first meeting with that Beloved of whom we have heard and read so much—courtship, not yet a betrothal, but a powerful reassurance that mystical marriage remains a possibility. In earlier centuries, the prescribed steps for arranged nuptials included a series of meetings between the young people, gift exchanges, falling in love, joining hands, the engagement, and finally marriage. We have briefly sighted the Beloved, who has also offered us the ineffable gift of oneness with Itself, a gift of Love intended to elevate and transfigure us. In an act of passionate generosity, It has given all that It is to us, has left Itself utterly exposed, and now asks a gift of us in return—the gift of our total self-transformation. Such a gift would be the culmination of the purgative way that began with letting go of the sensory part of the soul and all else attached to the small self, our self-stripping. Further purgation will purify our hearts, our inner vision *en route*, so that we may enjoy future touches from the Beloved, and these more than momentarily.

We have all luxuriated in a hot tub or bath, leaning back half-asleep while any aches in our muscles or joints melted away, wishing the water would stay warm and healing forever. A sighting of the Beloved is like this. We want to repose in such delight always, but that is when we have to remind ourselves that revelations are occasional and meant to highlight the difference between washed and unwashed, clean and unclean. If we remain submersed, the water will grow tepid and our efforts lazy. We need to rouse ourselves and resume our work. If our commitment has been tepid as well, the brief appearance of That our heart desires should be the hydrotherapy we need to restore zeal to our practices. Renewed commitment and stabilization of the gains from this breakthrough become the immediate targets and next steps of our ongoing preparation. Katherine Dowling Singh offers this explanation:

> One experience in an expanded level of consciousness, no matter how profound and no matter how permanently embedded in consciousness, usually does not in and of itself raise the level of consciousness. ... It appears that stability at the next ... level of consciousness is a consequence of time spent, balanced and centered, living at that level. .... Because the levels of consciousness [are] a hierarchy, the preceding level must be stabilized before one can move permanently beyond it into the next unfolding.[17]

How long we spend "stabilizing" in the meadow depends on two factors. Spirit knows our capabilities, how much ego annihilation we can handle at any given step of the way, and the ideal pace for us to advance.

The other factor flows from the human side. The mountain meadow is a place of great gladness, such that many seekers feel that have reached their goal of union with the Godhead. We also may feel we have achieved a high level of psychological togetherness within ourselves, that our newfound awareness is genuine. We have attained a heightened perception of physical creation as well. We feel whole and at peace.

We have in fact reached the pinnacle of what is sometimes called *the first mystic life*. But illumination, the glow flowing from our brief contact with the Godhead, is more precisely an *indication* of spiritual *growth*. It is not *completion*. It is a common experience among those still very much on the way, so much so that Evelyn Underhill characterized the state of illumination as *the largest and most densely populated province of the mystic kingdom*.

---

[17] Katherine Dowling Singh, *The Grace in Dying*, (San Francisco: HarperCollins, 1998), p. 255-6

We will meet many unfamiliar travelers here above the tree line. They will have emerged from other, innumerable, forest paths, the thickets of competing creeds and spiritual traditions and cultures. Above the tree line, as we draw nearer the Godhead and shed our different lifelong beliefs, the trails to the summit tend to merge. Yes, some of us still search for the *personal* God, while others seek to enter the Void, but even these apparently contrary paths will come together at the top of Mystic Mountain, there where nothing remains but That-Which-Is. Even those who long for *mystical marriage* must pass through the naughting darkness of the negative way to arrive at their nuptials.

Some travelers, after the hard work they've done to reach this level, may not care to go beyond it, and it's easy to understand why. We have known the divine, but the ego, albeit weakened, is still intact, still imagines itself somewhat separate from God. Moving on from this point and into the barrens, enduring the final purgation and total obliteration of the self is not, by comparison, a happy prospect. Bliss and contentment, and the personal experience of union with Love, if only for the duration of this one breakthrough, are powerful inducements to settle where we are. Life is good, prayer is good and nature has become a sacred playground. In contrast, the thought of total annihilation of that we consider to be us, of our entire being as we have known it up to this moment, can chill us to the core. Extraordinary courage is required to continue the climb into the high desert, which Evelyn Underhill called *the sorting house of the spiritual life. Here we part from the "nature mystics," the mystic poets, and all who shared in and were contented with the illuminated version of reality. Those who go on are the great and strong spirits, who do not seek to "know," but are driven to "be."*[18]

And so, we hesitate. Yet sound carries on a mountainside and we can hear voices from the peak conversing in accents that we recognize as our native speech, the language of our homeland. As much as we may wish to tarry in the meadow,

---

[18] Evelyn Underhill, *Mysticism*, 12th Edition, (New York: E. P. Dutton, 1961)

the initial impulse that started us on this pilgrimage still beckons to the hardiest and heartiest among us and we hope to be reckoned among Evelyn's *great and strong spirits*. Growth allows but the briefest breather for, as Augustine recognized, *the human heart cannot know rest until it rests in Thee.*

> Here there begins an eternal hunger, which shall never more be satisfied; it is an inward craving and hankering of ... the created spirit after an Uncreated Good. And since the spirit longs for fruition, and is invited and urged thereto by God, it must always desire its fulfillment. ... Here are great dishes of food and drink, ,,, but full satisfaction in fruition is the dish which is lacking, and therefore this hunger is ever renewed. ... Rivers of honey, full of all delights, flow forth ... but all this is in a creaturely way and below God, and hence there remains an eternal hunger and impatience. Though God gave to such a man all the gifts possessed by all the saints, and everything that He is able to give, but withheld Himself, the gaping desire of the spirit would remain hungry and unsatisfied, ... for the Spirit of God hunts our spirit: and the more it touches it, the greater our hunger and our craving. And this is the life of love in its highest working.[19]

The determined pilgrim, therefore, is not long delayed in the meadow, as enjoyable as it is. We have become intensely conscious of the Godhead we seek, yet are also mindful that our spirits are not yet even betrothed to the Beloved, let alone espoused.

It is most important to be free of major, nonspiritual commitments here. Those monks and nuns dedicated to the contemplative life, those "civilians" who've finished childrearing or retired from the workplace and those sharing life with a partner who is also traveling the mystic way obviously are in a more advantageous place from which to resume the climb toward the summit—for the remaining journey will demand all that we have to give.

Before we set out for these higher climes, however, we will discover that the nature of our practices and of our prayer and

---

[19] Jan Van Ruysbroeck, *The Adornment of Spiritual Marriage,* 2.53

meditation undergo a sea change, the first of many inner adjustments meant to prepare us for the coming of Love and the passive way. Our practice shifts more toward attitude—toward mindsets of service, ever deepening surrender, and (fair warning) suffering—with less emphasis on measurable activities. Meditation also undergoes a transformation into increasingly deeper experiences of infused contemplation. We might think of these changes as the ropes and poles and other tools we need for the final ascent towards the summit.

Service

The third of the four main Hindu yogas is *karma yoga*, union through selfless action One form this can take is service to others, a powerful tool to redirect the small self out of itself. There is also service at a higher level, the level of union with God's own benevolence, to be explored in a later chapter.

Service is a way to diminish the role of ego in our lives by placing the small self in settings where it will be less full of itself and more concerned with the needs of others. We learn humility and discover our ordinariness when we let others cut in line ahead of our egos. Selfless service can take the form of *practice*, a regularly scheduled routine like dishing up lunch at the homeless shelter every Thursday. It is also a readiness, an unconditional availability to others, a spontaneous willingness to do what needs to be done in the moment, whenever and wherever and whoever, however and as often as need presents itself. We perform service with no thoughts about outcomes, no attachment to results.

A particular saint of selflessness comes to mind, the young Dutch woman Etty Hillesum, who served her Jewish community in many small ways during the days of Nazi occupation, then continued her mission of aid and consolation at Auschwitz until it was her turn to enter the showers. Living in the shadow of daily oppression, in uncertainty from one hour to the next, she took to heart the admonition to give no thought for the morrow.

> The things that have to be done must be done, and for the rest, we must not allow ourselves to become infested with thousands of petty fears and worries, so many notions of no

confidence in God. ... Ultimately, we have just one moral duty: to reclaim large areas of peace in ourselves ... and to reflect it towards others. And the more peace there is in us, the more peace there also will be in our troubled world.[20]

Service changes the fundamental nature of work. It becomes free of ego when we work with no need for recognition, no need to blow our trumpets at the door of the temple. Nor do we use the results of our effort to pad our false identity. This is the true *Opus Dei*, the Work of God, in which the right hand knows not what the left hand is doing.

> Creating, yet not possessing,
> Working, yet not taking credit.
> Work is done, then forgotten.
> Therefore it lasts forever.
> —Lao Tzu

I wrote earlier that one of the marks of an authentic teacher or guru is that he or she comes to serve, not to *be* served or praised or pedestaled. This is the suffering servant of Isaiah, or the model held up to us by Paul: *(Jesus) did not regard equality with God as something to be exploited, but emptied himself* (Philippians, 2:6-7).

Self-sacrifice and service are marks of enlightenment. We could go so far as to say that ultimate fulfillment comes in giving one's life in service to others. A prevalent philosophy in the modern world is Ayn Rand's "objective self-interest," which ultimately proved unsatisfying even to her. What I'm describing here might be called *"enlightened* self-interest," for in meeting the needs of others we also benefit ourselves. If we wish to become conduits of Grace, then sharing Grace with others fulfills our need as well as theirs.

The Law, or Torah, of the Bible can be summed up as a vision of oneness—oneness with God and oneness with our neighbor. *Love the lord your God with your whole heart ... and your neighbor as yourself.* We each have particular gifts or capabilities to share, perhaps something as basic as being a

---

[20] *An Interrupted Life: the Diaries of Etty Hillesum 1941-43*, (New York: Washington Square Books, 1985), p. 229.

good listener. John Milton said of his blindness, *they also serve who only stand and wait.* Part and parcel of gift-sharing is humility, non-attachment, giving without thought of personal profit or praise or expectation of receiving a gift in return—in other words, removing ego from the equation.

If we are to experience self-fulfillment, our spirituality must shine through our unique God-given talents. In Native American terms, we must rediscover our *original medicine.* All that we are, whatever talents we have received, have been given so we might help those with whom we share creation and to further the evolution of this creation. My wife, for example, in addition to her ability as an author, has been given gifts of insight abetted by her training in counseling and spiritual direction, gifts that enable her to serve as a healer and consoler to those in pain, and as an advisor to spiritual seekers. Other endless examples of service flood the imagination: sheltering a stranger, picking up trash on the daily walk, recycling, medical skills, saving homes on fire, inspiring one's coworkers, manufacturing a reliable and affordable product, helping customers with problems, growing and processing healthful foods, yak herding, entertaining people with one's talent for putting a basketball through a hoop or striking out a batter, or a knack for acting ... the list is infinite and whether or not these actions are self-serving or offer service to others is a matter of our intention and attitude as we perform them.

One of the most powerful forms of service is to sit with and care for the dying—serving a person who can't stand or walk, can't form coherent thoughts or is incontinent, with the attendant loss of dignity. I recently helped my wife do this as well as she shepherded her 62-year-old "baby" sister through the final stages of cancer, changing her diapers as when she was a year old, constantly cleansing, laundering, making up and remaking her bed, dressing, cooking for and feeding her sister—chores that were nonstop and kept her on call day and night and in the middle of the night for months. It was a heartrending time and a blessed opportunity to serve.

Service often translates into surrender, asking time and energy from us that we might rather spend otherwise, that we set aside a project we would rather be doing, that we submit our ego, perhaps, to the head of a nonprofit agency, that we release our preferences and biases. Service asks that we surrender not only our time, but also our talents and often our tokens (money). Surrendering the ego's preferences, as we well know by now, is fundamental for its dissolution.

A deeper surrender

> Be thou thy self in thy whole Person the Sacrifice of a whole Burnt Offering, ascending in a Sacred flame of heavenly love to God, the only and eternal Beauty.
> —Peter Sterry

Surrender, we discovered early in our journey, is an active process, an activity in which we take part willingly and with our full being. It is not merely a passive acceptance of God's will in all that comes our way, for example, nor is it in any sense a giving up. We do not die to life when we surrender, but quite the opposite. We discover what it means to be wholly invested in life from a place of transcendence.

We can start by letting go of past regrets and successes, of future hopes, fantasies and concerns about events that may never happen. In this way, we release the illusion of fleeting time and finite space, basic forms of dualism. Our goal in this effort is that expressed in the title of Richard Alpert's (Ram Dass') famous little book: *Be Here Now*—to live like a good existentialist completely in the moment, where claims of urgency and constriction do not exist (but *eternity* and *infinity* do).

Here can be any "where," wherever we are at this instant; *now* is just this millisecond. Sight, taste, touch and all the senses become involved actors, not mere receptors, and consequently ignite our vitality. Living in the present, outside the enclosure of ordinary time, is that sensation you feel when you're crunching through autumn leaves, completely attuned to their dryness and the crackling beneath your boot, or the undivided attention you give to the smell and flavor and temperature of the soup in your spoon, unburdened by any judgment or preconception—an instant crystallized.

Normally our nature is not to live in the nakedness of the moment, but when we do, we open our hearts to life as it truly is, in this heartbeat, neither more nor less, devoid of past or future insinuation. Awareness of the moment is vitally important, we discover, because right now I am in exactly the place God wants me to be, the place I need to be for my growth. Yes, discerning what each instant has to teach us is no doubt difficult initially. But we can form the habit through repetition, simultaneously learning for just this moment to release our conflicts and battles and the passions they arouse, coming fully to rest in the now. It is only in the now, in the timeless zone, that we awaken to the reality of the world and imbibe the lessons and energy connected to that reality.

Our memories of past events, those more-or-less accurate links to gone time, are crammed like wall-to-wall metal bookshelves in hospitals, row-after-row of binders and records of former illness or health, which we further categorize into good/bad experiences, happy/sad experiences and the like. Lao Tzu referred to the visible, ever-changing universe as the *10,000 things*, upon which Thomas Merton commented, *if I am going to have a true memory, there are a thousand things that must first be forgotten.* The anonymous author of the Cloud of Unknowing had the same advice for his (or her) student: *Forget, forget, forget.*

In past years, we added to our stock of knowledge, trying to learn something new every day. As we approach the *negative way*, however, addition gives way to subtraction, learning surrenders to unlearning, complexity to simplification. We release our store of unnecessary information as part of giving up our coping tools and the disguises we've adopted to deal with past pain or to ward off potential future pain.

The synapses linking our memories are not going to dissolve and our memory banks don't empty just because we want them to, of course. And earlier on the path, as part of gaining self-knowledge, we deliberately reviewed our youthful years, trying to gain a larger perspective on the pattern of our lives. The process of *forgetting*, then, is not so much a matter of *losing* our memory as it is shifting our focus into the here and now.

When we immerse ourselves in this instant, memory becomes incidental; we transcend it and even our need to remember, though our past accumulation will continue to impact our present. For example, if we have overcome some brokenness in our past, the present moment will contain and reflect our gratitude. In the now, however, we can finally escape the duality inherent in the time-space continuum. Remembering gives way to simply being.

Similarly, our daydreams of the future, while they may initially launch us in one direction or another, typically fade or change shape as life takes a different course than we planned. Worries about what might, or might not, happen usually prove to be a waste of valuable energy. This is the *tyranny of the next day* that Søren Kierkegaard warned against. Be free of care like the birds, he said, that neither sow, nor reap, nor gather into barns, *get rid of the next day, and thus you are without the anxiety of self-torment.* Be here, now. Be flexible. Lose the wristwatch in a dresser drawer.

> When the mind is full of memories and preoccupied by the future, it misses the freshness of the present moment. In this way, we fail to recognize the luminous simplicity of mind that is always present behind the veils of thought.
> —Matthieu Ricard

While we're at it, we can break free as well of the tyranny of the *present* day with its planned sequence of activities. We can learn to listen closely, with our whole being, to what each moment of the day is asking of us. Living in the timeless zone is not easy, and in fact may be the most difficult practice we undertake, yet it is essential to our progress. For example, I've often found myself resisting the period set aside for daily prayer because it feels like time *stolen* from the *perceived* busyness of the rest of my day. Tasks and the time I will need to finish them invade the prayer hours, and this in spite of being "retired" and unharnessed from any sort of schedule. Chores insist they have higher priority than contemplation, perhaps because when I'm *merely sitting*, I'm *doing* "nothing." This kind of mental agitation makes us appreciate how living in the timeless zone can only happen through a tectonic shift in consciousness.

Freeing ourselves from the dualism of time presents us with a new and refreshing vision and offers another way to imagine timelessness. All time and all eternity are simultaneously present in the now moment. In this sense, for example, we can pray for those (like our parents) who preceded us in birth, even before they were born—a notion also implied in the modern theory of relativity and "overlapping time." When we collapse time like this, we move ourselves and other nearer to transcending it. Likewise, when we discover there is no place but *here*, we realize it contains every space that has ever existed, as well as the "outside existence." In a word, *here* is identical to the kingdom of heaven which is "among us," as near as God Itself, a celestial way of *being*, rather than a place.

Surrender also means releasing our will, even the hopes we foster about our spiritual advancement. This is more futurizing, and our longing for union with the Godhead is another offering we can lay upon our inner shrine. Still not much more than children on the mystical way, we may one day see that we haven't enough years, can never *do* enough or be passionate enough in this pursuit, receive sufficient Grace, or that the divine intention may not even be for us to reach the highest plateaus of contemplative prayer. John of the Cross warned against any such presumption, *For God does not bring to contemplation all those who purposely exercise themselves in the way of the spirit, not even half. Why? He best knows* (*The Dark Night*, 1.9.9). And so, here again, we must surrender to God's plan and pace, even to the possibility that we may advance no further than this day towards divine union, that we simply may lack the strength and capacity to do so.

> Those who are very weak, [God] keeps in this night [of the senses] for a long time. Their purgation is less intense and their temptations abated, and he frequently refreshes their senses to keep them from backsliding. They arrive at the purity of perfection late in life, and some of them never reach it entirely, for they are never wholly in the night or wholly out of it. ... Thus, God purges some individuals who are not destined to ascend to so lofty a degree of love as are others.[21]

---

[21] John of the Cross, *The Dark Night*, 1.14.5 and 2.1.1

When Spirit seems silent, we can only go about our daily tasks and practice and wait patiently for Its next move, if there is to be a next move.

The trek, nonetheless, is worth making. Ultimate Reality is like a stone thrown into the center of a pond, resonating as deeply as the leap of Basho's frog. We might compare the great contemplatives to the most clearly-formed ripples nearest to the stone. Our efforts, in turn, can replicate theirs, even if it turns out that we more closely resemble the less-defined ripples at the water's edge.

When we gaze upward from the base of Mystic Mountain, imagining these transfigured beings from afar, it may seem we will never be able to join them or share their rarified air. Yet those who have survived to the summit demonstrate the Self-realization latent within us. They've cleared trails and stacked cairns of spiritual wisdom to guide us. Whether we reach the summit or not, each bit of upward progress will open us to greater serenity and authenticity, grow our souls, free us from the *quiet desperation* that drives so many lives, and deepen the joy we feel from each taste of That-Which-Is.

I should add that John was more hopeful in other passages of *The Dark Night* than he was in this last quotation. As a spiritual director, he no doubt would have counseled us, in our present state, to persevere, be patient, trust God and be not afflicted. Nonetheless, as we enter the darkness of unknowing, and seeing how far we remain separated from the Godhead despite all our efforts and many years in search of the Beloved, can be a source of suffering to the soul—suffering that every master of the mystic way agrees is a necessary component of surrender and the path to Love.

Understanding suffering

> The Lord is close to the brokenhearted;
> Those whose spirit is crushed, he will save.
> —Psalm 34

Suffering can be overt or covert. Visible suffering can take many forms: chronic physical or mental illness, emotional loss or disappointment, frustration at our inability to control our destiny, natural disasters such as tsunamis or hurricanes.

Mankind's insanity is another major cause of suffering: the devastations of war, genocide, murder, greed and abuse in all its guises—the sum of which are chronicled for us daily in the evening news and cannot help but arouse immense universal sadness.

Even if we do not suffer overtly, there are incomprehensible areas inside our subconscious minds, the shadowy corners of our inner landscapes where we mortals constantly endure, silently and invisibly, what is generally called the human condition—our inheritance of illusion, attachments, unfulfilled aspirations, false ideas of who we are, false agendas, false images of reality, believing these false ideas—what Buddhists sum up in the term *samsara*, the fundamental condition of earthly existence. Christians might equate this hole in our spirits, our innate frailty, to *original sin*.

So long as we are in our bodies, we are susceptible to suffering. Life-altering accidents and events can happen at any time and with no warning. We are constantly at odds with what we deem right or wrong, too much or too little, with what rubs us the wrong way, with what we want versus what we have. Our governments declare war on crime, war on drugs, war on poverty, war on pollution, war on inequality. Every problem, it seems, must become a war, in both our personal and political arenas, and with little chance of victory. The usual result of war is to add to the overall suffering in the world, for invariably everyone loses.

What, then, are we to do about suffering? None of us, at the level of the ego, deliberately opens to pain. The usual, and perfectly normal, instinct is to protect ourselves from hurt, to do all in our power to maintain the status quo and avoid disruptive change. Suffering alarms us, dislocates our lives, and springs at us unexpectedly from surprising angles. We despair and experience a thousand fears, yet the more we resist suffering, the worse it becomes. What, then, is its purpose in our lives, what has it to do with surrender, and where can we see divine intent in pain?

Remember, my dears, that we are on a course to transform and destabilize the ego, and suffering is but one more of its complaints. Sufferings are the switchbacks on the ascent of Mystic Mountain. We seem to make little or no progress as we wind back and forth across the mountain's face, and constantly appear to be thrown back upon our small selves. But without suffering of our own, we might never experience, even in a small way, the pain that weighs down much of humanity. We might be unaware of karmic debt carried down from a previous existence and of work still to be done. Nor could we learn to transcend suffering and its inherent dualism. Unless we accept suffering as a necessary prelude to progress, unless we embrace it gratefully for the growth latent within it, unless we can transmute pain by awakening to the higher awareness it offers, we can never be free of it.

Birth, deterioration, death and rebirth is the cycle all creation follows. The seeds must drop from the fading plant and die before they can germinate and create new shoots. Nature generates order from disorder, disintegration through entropy and transformation from death as immutably as it drives the seasonal round. This is the lesson hidden in the cross. This is the dance of Lord Shiva on the bowed back of humanity and we had best learn to join the dance and revel in its rhythms.

> You don't ask what a dance means, you enjoy it. You don't ask what the world means, you enjoy it. You don't ask what you mean, you enjoy yourself ... But to enjoy the world requires something more than mere good health and good spirits, for this world ... is horrendous. *All life*, said the Buddha, *is sorrowful*; and so, indeed, it is—life consuming life. ... *The world*, said the Buddha, *is an ever-burning fire*. And so it is. And that is what one has to affirm with a yea! A dance!
>
> —Joseph Campbell

The Sufis teach that our *task is to transform suffering into joy*, which, by the way, is a common theme in the hagiographies of saints. We are speaking now of the suffering that enlarges us, suffering viewed in the immense context of eternity rather than boxed within the limited framework of the ego. We are wounded in the greater sense not to make us smaller, but to open us to kindness. Suffering is the iconoclast that shatters the icons of false self and illusion. It shakes us out of complacency, grabs us by the napes of our necks and hurls us into the immediacy of now. Here, we are ripped open and our deepest fears abruptly displayed. Suffering forces us to admit that we simply cannot avoid some trials.

Again we are asked to surrender, actively surrender, to participate in our hurting and welcome it as part of Love's plan to peck apart the shell of ego from within and birth the larger Self gestating within. During World War II, before she was shipped to Auschwitz, Etty Hillesum wrote in her diary:

> I am in Poland every day. ... I often see visions of poisonous green smoke; I am with the hungry, with the ill-treated and the dying every day, but I am also with the jasmine and with that piece of sky beyond my window; there is room for everything in a single life, for belief in God and for a miserable end. ... It is a question of living life from minute-to-minute and taking suffering into the bargain. And it is no small bargain these days. But does it matter if it is the Inquisition that causes people to suffer in one century and war and pogroms in another? ... Suffering has always been with us. Does is really matter in what form it comes? All that matters is how we bear with it and how we fit in into our lives. ... It sounds paradoxical: by excluding death from our life, we cannot live a full life, and by admitting death into our life, we enlarge and enrich it.[22]

When we embrace suffering as Etty did, we discover the blessing concealed within it. We can resolve to bear it as best we can, to find the center of equilibrium within it, the balance that will lighten its burden, and yes, to shoulder it like a sweet yoke. Imitating the resilient reed, we can bend to the tempest of suffering without breaking. The unyielding tree is the one that fractures and shatters, loses its limbs and uproots in the storm.

Recall the earlier quotation from Milarepa. If we see our suffering as a *demon*, if our ego becomes addicted to it and

---

[22] *An Interrupted Life: the Diaries of Etty Hillesum 1941-43*, (New York: Washington Square Books, 1985), pp. 159, 162

allows it to become our newest identity, we only add to its power. If we see it as our *father and mother*, our loving teacher, if we can hear what it's trying to tell us, we can free ourselves from its grip the moment we have absorbed that lesson. We emerge from suffering purified of ego, as gold tried in the fire.

> To hold together in one thought those terrible opposites of good and evil which struggle in the world is to be capable of life, and only love will hold them so. Our labor, like Job's labor, is to learn through suffering to love ... to love even that which lets us suffer.
>
> —Archibald MacLeish

A deceased friend owned an ivory statue of a Buddha with one thousand hands and an eye in the palm of each hand. As the story goes, this Buddha was about to enter nirvana when he heard of a person still suffering on earth. Given the choice between nirvana and helping that person, he chose to help. Immediately he entered nirvana, but was given a thousand hands so he could reach out to those in need and an eye in each hand so he might see through to the heart of their sorrow.

This particular Buddha illustrates just how suffering burns away ego. As in the case of Etty Hillesum, it awakens us to compassion and kindness towards others, for seeping from our own wounds is empathy with their woundedness as well. We cannot bear to see them hurting in the same way we hurt, and our hearts long to pour out love on all our broken companions and to do whatever we can to alleviate their misery. When one member of our universal family is hurting, we all hurt. On the other hand, kindness and compassion can literally transform the lives of the suffering.

> Believe me, if there were a man willing to suffer on account of God and God alone, then he fell a sudden prey to the collective sufferings of all the world, it would not trouble him nor bow him down, for God would be the bearer of his burden.
>
> —Meister Eckhart

This is the healing balance within our hearts. We are utterly individual and at the same time intimately linked to every feature of the cosmos, not just its physical particles, but its mental, emotional and spiritual dimensions as well—all of creation's body-mind-soul-spirit. The web comprised of us connected beings shudders at each disturbance, just as a spider's entire web shudders at the impact of a fly. The affairs of all beings are internal affairs. Thus it is also true that, through our interconnectedness, if we *relieve* the aching of one among us, we ease the hurting of all. *When one flower blooms, it is spring everywhere.* This is one aspect of the Bodhisattva mentality, of which we'll say more in a later chapter.

Interconnectedness carries with it a profounder responsibility as well, which is shared *culpability* for all the harmful actions of humankind, the human causes of suffering. In a sense, this means to practice Christ consciousness, for like the Christ, we take on the "sin" and ignorance of all humanity. Falling (and rising again) is fundamental to the human condition, and when one falls, we are all pulled down. An artery may be blocked with plaque, but every cell, every organ and muscle in the body, suffers as a result. Conversely, when one of us rises again, all are uplifted. *When one flower blooms, it is spring everywhere.*

Regina Sara Ryan, in her book *Igniting the Inner Life*, tells the story of Dr. Ihaleakala Hew Len, a prison psychologist in Hawaii. Practicing a form of Ho'OPonopono, an ancient Hawaiian tradition of reconciliation and forgiveness, he studies the files of criminally insane inmates. Interiorizing and taking on full responsibility for each of their illnesses, he then heals them by extending love and forgiveness to himself. Without further therapeutic counseling, these prisoners begin to seek peace and self-understanding.[23]

> Compassionate toward yourself,
> you reconcile all beings in the world.
> —Lao Tzu

Taking the pain of another into our own interior and treating it as if it were our own can lead to healing of their

---

[23] Regina Sara Ryan, *Igniting the Inner Life,* (Prescott: Hohm Press, 2010) pp. 191-2.
(See also the website http://www.idreamcatcher.com/hooponopono)

suffering. Many parents would gladly do so for their children. To pray that we be given the earache tormenting a 4-year-old is far different, however, than asking, *give my spouse's cancer to me.* If we make such a request, we take on a tremendous burden, one that may overwhelm our faith as well as our physical and emotional resources. We don't know the divine intent in all this suffering, whether we are meant to assume such a weight or not, and we are faced here with a classic example of the admonition, *be careful what you wish for.* As in every prayer, every form of surrender, the bottom line is ... *if it be your will. Thy will be done in every circumstance.*

Cosmic Prayer and Beginning Contemplation

Earlier we likened the spiritual ascent to a spiraling upward journey. Besides leading us up the mountain, the spiral is also an ancient symbol of the path to the center of our being. The circling path keeps returning us to the same views, but each time from a higher perspective. If I seem to repeat myself as we continue our climb, it is hopefully, with each pass, from this loftier view.

The universal priesthood

Spoken prayer is one such example. When we offer praise and thanksgiving from a higher perspective and lay our petitions before the Godhead, we represent all humankind and all creation, for we now *know* that we are one and interconnected with all this being. Lingering doubts may suggest that we cannot possibly embrace the entire world in our prayer, but God certainly can. Besides, it is no longer we who pray, but rather, Love that prays within us. As It animates us from within, we become the one who offers, as well as the offering and That which receives the offering, with the whole of existence gathered in our hearts. We become what the apostle Peter called *living stones in a spiritual house and holy priesthood ... a chosen race, a kingly priesthood.* In the fifth century, Leo the Great sermonized that all believers are anointed and consecrated priests by the Holy Spirit and asked what could be more priestly than offering the sacrifice of a clear conscience on the altar of the heart (*Sermon 4*)? In such prayer, we are all, women and men, *priests forever, of the order of Melchizedek.*

Another summons that comes to us in the relative calm of illumination is an invitation to deepen our prayer. It's easy to wonder, particularly if all is well with us, *if I am on the spiritual path, where is that suffering of which I've read? Shouldn't I be experiencing more hardship in my search?* Don't worry, trials will come as we resume our climb from the meadow. But we can take advantage of the tranquility of this interlude to open ourselves to the inner workings of Love in our prayer.

From meditation to contemplation

> The mind weighs and measures
> but it is the spirit
> that reaches the heart of life
> and embraces the secret;
> and the seed of the spirit is
> deathless.
> —Khalil Gibran

Until now, we have prayed and meditated *actively*, focusing our thoughts and imagination using a theme or quotation from our spiritual reading, a prayer guide, or similar inspiration. This was not a silencing of the mind, but deliberate mental centering, putting the intellect to work to explore specific themes. Through personal self-discipline we also learned to direct our faculties inward towards our center during active recollection, perhaps while repeating a mantra. This has been admirable work.

Now the time has arrived to move from thought-full to thought-less prayer, time to penetrate our immense, interior solitude, to abandon language and ideas and sink into silence. In the inner abyss our only activity is to trust the Godhead who dwells there to meet us more than halfway and to instill in us the wisdom that surpasses human understanding, the secret knowledge infused by Love. Bede Griffiths, a Benedictine monk who lived most of his years in India, described contemplation as *knowledge by love*.

> It reaches out to the infinite and the eternal. ... It is not something we achieve for ourselves; it is something that comes when we let go. We have to abandon everything, all

words, thoughts, hopes, fears, all attachment to ourselves or to any earthly thing, and let the divine mystery take possession of our lives.[24]

The unknown author of *The Cloud of Unknowing* and *The Book of Privy Counsel* wrote that our only activity as we advance beyond the initial forms of prayer should be *a naked intent reaching out towards God.* Initially God comes to us robed in the many guises mankind has attributed to him: goodness, kindness, omnipotence, power, might. But all of these concepts can be wrapped up and *hidden*, in the author's words, *in the word 'is.'* Being then appears *naked*, devoid of concepts, deeper than salvation or creation, as a blind stirring of Love. When we approach That-Which-Is we must be similarly stripped. The anonymous writer continued:

> Unclothe your awareness of analytical thoughts. Keep it empty. Don't cogitate on yourself or on others ... let them go. ... You no longer need to feed your mind by meditating on who you are and who God is. You're past that, although it helped you once. These meditations filled your mind and taught you about God. Through them, you gained spiritual wisdom. But now you need to change direction, seek God a different way. ... No name, no emotion, no thought is more like the everlasting nature of God than the experience you have, see, and feel in the blind and loving observation of the word *is*.[25]

In contemplation we can only achieve nakedness by releasing our preconceived notions, beliefs, the jangle of emotions and desires. We have to shed the ego we wear like a suit of armor against both the natural and supernatural worlds. This is what we do when we reach out to God with *naked intent*, to That-Which-Is also reaching out to us. Our basic stance is an act of patient, emptied longing.

---

[24] Bede Griffiths, *Inner Directions Journal*, (Inner Directions Foundation) Summer, 1996.
[25] Anonymous, *Book of Privy Counsel,* Chapter 5

Infused prayer

As the discursive form of meditation subsides and we settle into simple yearning for God stripped of *analytical thought*, we begin to experience *infused recollection*. We may have sensed it fleetingly before now, but after the breakthrough into the Godhead, it becomes the gateway for our entry into *contemplation*. Without our willing it and with no effort on our part, our attention remains centered for longer periods on the Being within. Recollection doesn't happen because we have taken the one seat and closed our eyes, or through any striving of the mind. In fact, any attempt to involve the intellect in this gentle inward focus, trying perhaps to understand the nature of it or "cooperate" with it, only disturbs it. Mental activity diverts us from any expansion, or any communication, that might otherwise be secretly transmitted within us. What we can do when this infusion occurs is rest gratefully in the divine presence in fond awareness and await further instruction. Love will let us know where we need to go next.

> Infused prayer, which is not the work of man, comes as a gift. A prayerful spirit comes and summons one down into the heart, just as one person might take another by the hand and draw him forcibly from one room into another. The soul is bound by an external force and remains willingly within while the prayerful spirit is with it.
> —Theophan the Recluse

Infused recollection, sometimes referred to as the *prayer of quiet*, the *prayer of silence*, or the *prayer of simplicity*, prepares us for loftier passive prayer yet to come. It sets us on the last of the four major Hindu paths to nondualism, the *Raja* (or "royal") *yoga*, union through ever-deepening contemplation. By advancing through the eight stages of Raja yoga envisioned in the Hindu scheme, the seeker not only is freed from dualism, but also achieves *samadhi*, union with the One. The Western mystical tradition likewise teaches that contemplation is the surest and most direct route to Oneness.

As the old saw says, don't just *do* something; *sit* there! This is prayer as *underachievement*, an elemental shift away from the world's notion of progress, the need to make each moment *productive*. Over time, as we learn to release our reliance on the mind, we develop growing stability in our prayer that engenders a movement from *doing* to simply *being*. I'm reminded of a friend's grandfather, a man in his nineties, who had an incredible capacity to sit silently, passing his entire day wrapped in a blanket in any easy chair enjoying idle tranquility, eyes closed, but not asleep, getting up only to toilet or eat and at bedtime. If someone spoke to him, he responded coherently, although his words were weighty and few. He seemed the epitome of *rock solid*, the unshakable one seat.

The most vivid impression felt during infused prayer is the deep presence of the Godhead, now only partially-concealed within us. Our natural instinct is to hold our bodies as motionless as possible, lest the slightest movement create what would feel like massive disruption. Our breath becomes so slow and shallow that the rise and fall of our chest is hardly noticeable. We might worry that any thought will create major turbulence, although, to our surprise, thinking is not a real concern in this silence. We can't even form thoughts intentionally because each potential "sentence" is blocked before it gets past a couple of words. We are incapable of deliberation.

With regular practice our breathing settles into a steady rhythm, honing us for the influx of Love, the breakthrough into the next level of awareness. With each in-spiration, we sense Spirit entering from outside our bodies. With each ex-spiration, Spirit exits, carrying off any negativity we may have suppressed within us. Our breathing, the slow inward and outward movement of our lungs and diaphragm, becomes a swinging door reflecting the inflow and outflow of Love.

When we began to practice meditation, our minds may have been as chaotic as bar scenes in old westerns where pandemonium, smoke, noise and turmoil raged in dimly-lit rooms and men in semi-drunken stupors groped for flouncy barmaids in provocative tutus. But we eventually tired of this bedlam and longed for our thoughts to settle. We needed help and like Rûmî, we filed our complaint: *Whoever brought me to this tavern will have to take me home* and now help arrives. As we inhale, Love enters like the hero in the white hat pushing through the swinging doors of the bar, and Its presence alone stills the room. Then, as we exhale, off It goes again, taking a couple of the rowdies (and our confusion) with It. Synchronized to our breathing, Love comes and goes, comes and goes.

As we look even more closely at this swinging door, we realize that the door and the wall dividing outside from inside is but another Hollywood façade, another illusion designed to create a sense of separation where none exists. Inside-outside, both the same, as are Spirit's coming and going.

> When you make the two one, when you make the inner as outer and the outer as inner, then shall you enter the kingdom.
> —*The Gospel of the Beloved Companion*

During silent prayer, as we release ourselves to Love within us and enveloping us, our bodies seem to *melt* into their setting, into the chair, into the room, into the surrounding air—and furthermore, the setting itself seems to dissolve, until the only presence felt is the Spirit of Love. We can't even say that where we end, Spirit begins, for there is no end or beginning. When this happens, when the body and mind dissolve into the omnipresent Divinity, an energetic force within us is freed. Teresa of Avila described its flow as follows:

> It seems as if there are in my head many rushing rivers and that these waters are hurtling downward, and many little birds and whistling sounds, not in the ears but in the upper part of the head where, they say, the higher part of the soul is. And I was in that superior part for a long time, for it seems this powerful movement of the spirit is a swift upward one.[26]

A Hindu might smile at Teresa's simplistic description of her experience. After all, Hinduism has made a science of *kundalini*, or serpent energy, and its flow from the base of the spine, up and down the dual channels of ida and pingula, spinning through the chakras situated where the channels intersect, and finally up into the crown chakra at the top of the head.

---

[26] Teresa of Avila, *The Interior Castle*, 4.10

This hidden, spiritual energy is known by different names in various cultures: the *tao* (power); the *chi* that practitioners of Tai Chi seek to unleash; *spirit* in our western world; the *orenda* of the Cree Indian; the ... *prana* liberated and fortified by yogic practices. It is symbolized in the medical caduceus: twin serpents (the *ida* and *pingula* of kundalini yoga) intertwined around the winged staff representing the spine and its ascending power centers, or *chakras*.[27]

The operation of this force is experienced by Christian mystics as the purifying fire of Love coursing through and cleansing, tempering and refining the body and the faculties of the mind and soul. Other cultures similarly view it as a vital and cathartic energy.

Some experience the energy as a burning sensation throughout the body, often focused in the heart center, during contemplation and sometimes, unexpectedly, in the course of the day. Perhaps this is why mystics speak of Spirit and Love as a consuming fire. Catherine of Genoa and Richard Rolle, among others, wrote of the *Fire of Love* (the title of Rolle's book) burning within their hearts. Walter Hilton and the author the *Cloud of Unknowing* also spoke of "sensible heat" as a common spiritual experience. While the latter two were dismissive of this sensation, Catherine and Richard welcomed its purging effect.

Spiritual sleep

As we sink into the silence of contemplation, we may enter a condition called *conscious sleep* or *spiritual sleep* or *yoga nitra*. The crossover point separating deep contemplation from deep sleep can be difficult to recognize until the snoring starts. But short of the heavy breathing, and although this condition feels much like sleep, we remain at least vaguely alert. We may feel paralyzed otherwise, however, unable to move, do anything, or think anything, locked into a state of suspension. This is a truly passive condition and we'll say more about it later when we look into prayers of rapture and ecstasy, when

---

[27] John Sack, *Yearning for the Father: The Lord's Prayer and the Mystic Journey*, (Prescott: Hohm Press, 2006), pp. 128-29

the soul and body seem to separate. For now, know that this sleep is a good thing because Love, rather than we, is at work and for its duration we verge on a nearness to God akin to union.

> The soul does not even find itself awake in order to love. But blessed sleep, happy inebriation that makes the Bridegroom supply what the soul cannot do, ... for while the faculties are dead or asleep, love remains alive. And the Lord ordains that the soul function so wonderfully, without its understanding how, that it is made one, in great purity, with the very Lord of love, who is God. For no one hinders the soul, neither senses nor faculties ... nor is the will aware of itself.[28]

In this state of conscious sleep, or in actual, unconscious sleep in one's bed, the body may go through additional preparation for the next breakthrough. Like the purring of a happy cat, toning currents vibrate through the entire frame, from head to sole, not just up and down the spine as with *kundalini energy*, perhaps accompanied by a rhythmic sound—steady drumbeats, for example. A mantra or prayer my repeat rapidly and for some time through what consciousness remains to the sleeper, *Thank you, thank you, thank you, thank you*, but even in that dim awareness, mind knows that it is not initiating this stream, that it emanates from a source subliminal or superior to thought.

Changes in prayer and attitude, plus the inclusiveness inherent in our broadened vision, prepare us for the next leg of our journey. It's time to leave the mountain meadow and climb to the dry and rocky barrens, the high desert where surrender, like a flowering cactus, will reach full bloom. The heat, as we will soon learn, is incinerating at this altitude. Shade, or any chance to hide from the Light, is nonexistent in this treeless waste. At times we may feel as heavy-legged as Frodo in *The Lord of the Rings*, trudging up Mount Doom with his oppressive and perilous cargo. We need help to continue and this is where the presence of Love is fully felt.

---

[28] Teresa of Avila, *Meditations on the Song of Songs*, 6.4

The interlude in the meadow has led us through the transition from our active role in self-transformation to passive growth, where we can only try our best not to interfere while Love reshapes us. Like the wandering Israelites, we will discover in the desert that we can no longer survive on our wits and resources. We must accept the daily manna, the quail and water—gifts of Love—if we are to endure. The active labors of Egypt are behind us. The slaveholders who pursued us have drowned in the sea of beginning contemplation, and the desert over time will free us from any lingering desire for the fleshpots our captors once set before us.

We resume our pilgrimage then, trying to set aside our natural inclination towards action so that Love can fulfill its *supernatural activity* within us (although this latter *doing* is more an *undoing* or a *nondoing* than anything we would call activity). Nil Sorski, a Russian hermit of the fifteenth century, said that as long as a person retains so much as a shred of belief that anyone or anything can help him, he or she will remain in the spiritual pit. This includes our own efforts, sheer luck or happenstance, and even faith in God.[29] Realizing and accepting our ultimate helplessness is the true turning point on the mystic way.

---

[29] Cited in Richard John Friedlander, *Paradise Besieged*, (Berkeley: Flying High Press, 2009), p. 120

Chapter 3. The High Desert

> O God, you are my God, for you I long;
> for you my soul is thirsting.
> My body pines for you
> like a dry, weary land without water.
> —Psalm 63

Wandering in wastelands and subjecting the spirit to desert extremes are common preludes to every great movement of Love. In the desert we feel lucky to survive. It forces us to abandon all but what we need to stay alive. Many great masters literally began their spiritual pursuit in the barrens. Emulating the Jewish people who wandered forty years in the desert before they could enter the land of promise, the Jewish prophets, John the Baptist and Jesus all retreated into the wilderness. Some, like the desert fathers and mothers of ante-Nicene Christianity, never left. The great ascetics of Hinduism and Buddhism likewise withdrew into forests and caves or simply wandered naked and homeless in search of ultimate Nakedness. Across the globe today, communities of monks and nuns from every faith tradition still flee voluntarily from the world.

When we head up this desolate stretch of our inner terrain, we do so because we understand that it leads to ever more profound stillness and stripping of the ego—as well as to ignorance (that is, ignore-ance) of the external world. Our aim, in a nutshell, is to shed every leftover bit of baggage preventing our full experience of That-Which-Is. Tossing our favorite belongings won't be easy, as we've surely discovered by now, because they include everything we've cherished about ourselves or fretted over until now, and every mask, disguise, coping mechanism and strategy that got us through the early years. It includes as well the nonspiritual aspects of every human connection we have so far failed to sublimate. No wonder our ego digs in its heels when it sees us turn towards the high desert.

The mystic way from this point actually consists not in *getting rid* of the ego, but rather allowing it to simply fade away, for it has never had any real substance. The small self has never been anything but a chimera we created, which raises the question: why do we cling to it so stubbornly? Phrased another way, how much of this illusory imposter are we willing to send packing to make room for our authentic Self, that Being who waits behind all our expressions of nonbeing?

Such questions remind me of a man whose wife died after fifty years of marriage. The widower went to live with his daughter who apologized the next morning because she hadn't burned his toast "the way he liked it." The man sighed and confessed that the day after their wedding his wife had been terribly distressed because she'd burned his toast and to spare her feelings he'd said, "That's actually how I prefer it." For fifty years he'd endured burnt toast, harassed by an illusion that he himself had created. Such is life in the grip of the ego.

Our goal here is not the destruction of our personalities, but to release their illusory aspects so that we can discover our true Self. We don't abandon our humanity, but hope to raise it to its highest expression—that fully-realized, God-filled, golden entity who is ever alive to the moment, spontaneous, compassionate, self-directed, free of fear and delusion, whose intentions and perceptions are focused and pure, the one who recognizes the sacredness of his or her being and that of others and burns with love for the Divine. Self-realization as humans predisposes us to God-realization. Individual awareness opens into cosmic awareness, into Christ-consciousness or Buddha-consciousness. Transcendent beings live not in their egos; rather, the Godhead works through them, using their bodies and minds to extend benevolence to all creation.

> The being-one with God demands of man that he is man; the experience must not, exclusively or by preference, aim at the Godhead; it must also—at the same time—be able to *taste* everything that belongs to the concrete, disconcerting ... Humanity."
>
> —Hadewijch

The Negative Way

In the desert, the *via negativa* or negative way, comes into full play. Unimaginable feats of asceticism and mortification are not the purpose of this way, however. Yes, we had to learn right intention and to purge our lowest urgings while we were in the forest, with a view toward one day transcending them, but following our breakthrough into Oneness, we discover that nothing created can encumber us or separate from the Godhead. Every object, including our bodies, and each event that transpires in our lives, only serves to point us towards the Divine. We see the cosmos with newly sensitized vision, as a cause not for troubling concern but for ecstasy. Mere asceticism, with its ego-stroking self-congratulation, only keeps us stuck in our small selves.

> The people most separated from God are the ascetics by their asceticism, the devotees by their devotion, and the knowers by their knowledge. ... I went to pray with the devotees, and did not feel in my place. I went among those who mortify themselves ... among those who fast, and still I did not feel in my place. I said, "O my God, what then is the way to thee?" And the answer given me was, "Abandon thyself and come."
>
> —Bâyazîd al-Bistâmî

All practices, whether we continue them or not, are secondary to seeking out the Godhead. We still have our physical needs, of course, and to satisfy them is natural. When we are hungry, we eat. When we are tired, we sleep. When we are cold or warm, we dress accordingly. But these superficial needs can be released with gratitude once satisfied. They need not become abiding distractions. If they attach to our hearts, they create obstacles to the inflow of Love. I visited Denmark as a young man where the Danes, with their fine self-deprecating humor, used to joke that their only topics of conversation were what they ate at their last meal or what they planned to eat at their next meal. Don't be like the Danes!

> To make an issue of the world amounts to turning yourself toward yourself; it is to pass your time struggling with yourself; it is to take account of your feelings and to remain with yourself against your concupiscence. ... In all truth, *asceticism is the ardent aspiration of the heart towards Him alone* [emphasis mine]; it is to place in Him the aspirations and desires of the soul; to be preoccupied

> uniquely with Him, without any other preoccupation, so that He (to whom be praise!) may remove the mass of these causes.
>
> —Ibn al-'Arif

Note that It is "He" who removes the burrs that still cling to us, and surprisingly they often do just fall away once they have served their purpose in awakening us. This is true not only of annoying, trivial habits, but also of compulsions, addictions and beliefs we once thought were hopelessly entrenched. Such is the impact of Love on our lives.

We will know suffering too, of course, a more refined suffering than we have yet experienced. The desert is a crucible in which we are purified by fire, the conflagration in which we finally incinerate any illusion, any *samsara*, still tingeing our awareness.

Rebirth in Spirit and Fire

> The love of God has been poured into our hearts
> through the Holy Spirit that has been given to us.
> —Romans, 5:5

> It seems to me the Holy Spirit must be a mediator between the soul and God, the One who moves it with such ardent desires, for he enkindles it in a supreme fire.
> —Teresa of Avila

Since the Author-of-all-that-is first breathed *Let there be ...* and the ticking of deep time began nearly fourteen billion years ago, Spirit has guided the evolution of the cosmic plan and the full flowering of consciousness. It will continue to do so until time ends, when the plan is complete. Spirit is the Alpha and Omega, the beginning and the end of the divine unfolding.

When primordial matter released its potential for life, life that eventually included us humans, Spirit joined in to further our growth, prehistorically in developing the physical organism, then leading us into rational behavior through our intellects, followed by the call to conscious soul work. In the end, It will guide us to the depths of our being where the Godhead awaits. Thus Spirit works in secret as it were, inviting us to set out on the journey to transcendence, hidden within us as an implanted mystery we must explore, acting as the agent of our transformation, the master gardener who oversees the pruning and fruition of the divine seed implanted from eternity. Just as we recognize the course of a mighty wind by observing leaning trees and blowing leaves, the movement of Spirit is seen in the fruits of Its passage.

> The spirit in man is the 'fine point of the soul,' ... the point of contact between the human and the divine. ... The spirit in man is a 'gift' or grace; it is the presence in us of the divine Spirit. When body and soul are moved by the Spirit, then the whole being of man is transfigured. This was the very purpose of creation from the beginning, that body and soul, matter and mind, man and the universe, might be moved by the Spirit and drawn into the divine light and life.[30]

The inpouring of Spirit into our hearts, referred to as Grace in all wisdom traditions, marks the next breakthrough on our ascent of Mystic Mountain. That-Which-Is breaks through into our hearts and when It has completed Its work, we will discover that we have broken through into It as well.

> This is ... the function of grace, namely to condition [humanity's] homecoming to the center from start to finish. It is the very attraction of the center itself ... that provides the incentive to start on the way and the energy to face and overcome its ... various obstacles. ... Grace is the welcoming hand into the center when man finds himself standing at long last on the brink of the great divide where all familiar human landmarks have disappeared.[31]

When we speak of Spirit from the Christian perspective, we are borrowing an image from fourth-century Church history, viewing God as a trinity of Father, Son and Holy Spirit (or Holy Ghost). This was generally seen as an all-male trinity, but the picture has shifted in recent years, linking the Holy Spirit to the female Wisdom figure of the Old Testament, and

---

[30] Bede Griffiths, *The Marriage of East and West*, (Springfield: Templegate Publishers, 1982), p.77
[31] Marco Pallis, "Is There Room for Grace in Buddhism?" in *Sword of Gnosis* (Penguin Metaphysical Library,1974)

consequently positing Spirit as the feminine aspect of the trinity. In Greek she is *Sophia,* in Latin, *Sapientia*—both female names—and in the Syriac tradition the Holy Spirit Itself was called Mother, with the infinite and reassuring capacity for birthing and nurturing that divine motherhood implies.

We were born in the waters of our mothers, perhaps were baptized also in water that symbolized our second birth into religion or have undergone ritual ablutions in sacred streams such as the Ganges. But John the Baptist carried such events one step further when he spoke of the Christ to come: "I baptize you with water. ... He will baptize you with the Holy Spirit and with *fire* (Luke 3:16). Jesus said of this rebirth, during his nighttime meeting with the Pharisee Nicodemus, *What is born of human nature is human. What is born of Spirit is spirit* (John 3:6).

Extending the imagery of fire, the Baptist added, *His winnowing fork is in his hand to clear his threshing floor and gather the wheat into his granary; but the chaff he will burn with an unquenchable fire* (Luke 3: 17). Baptism in Spirit is a baptism of fire, where our remaining attachments are consumed like chaff until in the end we are left with God alone. This purging by fire would have recalled for John's Jewish listeners the extraction of gold from the dross or alloy that lowered its value. The prophet Malachi said of God's messenger to come:

> Who will be able to resist the day of his coming? Who will remain standing when he appears? For he will be like a refiner's fire, like fullers' alkali. He will take his seat as refiner and purifier; he will purify the sons of Levi and refine them like gold and silver.
> —Malachi 3:2-3

In both *The Dark Night* and *The Living Flame of Love* John of the Cross similarly compared the soul, which sits between our senses and our spirit, to a piece of wood and the work of Spirit to a flame. Initially, the wood is wet and the fire must dry it before it will burn. This is the kindling stage before the purifying work of Spirit, the cleansing by fire, begins in earnest, when the wood and the air within the flame, which might be compared to the human spirit, are totally consumed and transformed into flame.

Not surprisingly, in the Biblical account of Pentecost, the Holy Spirit descended upon each apostle in the guise of a tongue of fire. Jesus' timorous followers were transformed by this mystical experience into the indomitable cadre of missionaries who revolutionized Western culture and spirituality. Finally, with the inpouring of divine wisdom, they understood what he had been trying to teach them during their several years together. Peter described another occurrence during which Spirit descended in the same fashion upon a group of gentiles (Acts 11:15). Then there is the story of the desert fathers, Abba Lot and Abba Joseph:

> Abba Lot went to see Abba Joseph and said to him, *Abba, I say my little office, I fast a little, I pray and meditate, I live in peace and, as far as I can, I purify my thoughts. What else can I do?*
>
> Then the old man stood up and stretched his hands towards heaven. His fingers became like ten lamps of fire and he said, *if you will, you can become all flame.*[32]

Another name for Spirit

The literature of mysticism uses numerous metaphors to describe Spirit based, one imagines, on how It was experienced by the authors—a mighty wind, purifying fire, living water, a combination of water and fire, and of course as divine Grace. Spirit appears in the Judeo-Christian scriptures in the form of a dove, as tongues of flame, and in the desert as a cloud by day and pillar of fire by night when It led the Israelites to the promised land.

What the mystic intuits in the course of this inpouring is another name for Spirit, the name we have used throughout this book, which is divine Love. In the earlier paragraph describing the role of Spirit in the evolution of the universe and

---

[32] Benedicta Ward, translator, *The Sayings of the Desert Fathers,* (Kalamazoo: Cistercian Publications, 1975), p. 103

human consciousness, we could substitute the word *Love* for *Spirit* throughout and it would be just as true.

> Since the Author-of-all-that-is first breathed *Let there be ...* and the ticking of deep time began nearly fourteen billion years ago, *Love* has guided the evolution of the cosmic plan and the full flowering of consciousness. ... *Love* is the Alpha and Omega, the beginning and the end, of the divine unfolding. When primordial matter released its potential for life, life that eventually included us humans, *Love* joined in to further our growth ... etc.

Love summons us to conscious soul work. Love is the lure that beguiles us at the time of our call. Love guides and encourages the transformation of the sensual part of our souls through our years of active practice. Love, more powerfully than renunciation or mortification, unclutters our hearts and prepares our spirits for transfiguration. And finally, in the moment we are united to the Beloved, we will understand that Love is who we eternally are AND who God eternally *is*.

Love is also implacable, *strong as death and relentless as hell* (Song of Songs, 8:6). It will sear us to the core, cauterizing the tumors in our souls, but we will welcome this surgery for we know it is transfiguring. Love consumes the very heart of our former self in a blaze that simultaneously burns out our impurities and—in proportion to our preparedness and willingness to surrender to Its working—transforms us into Itself.

> Whosoever shall be sore wounded by love
> will never become whole save he embrace
> the self-same love that wounded him.
> —Mechthild of Magdeburg

Imagine for a moment that in the darkness of night you are being led to a beach bordering the boundless ocean of bliss. There on the shore a ghostly figure is tossing all of your files into a bonfire—your birth certificate, school transcripts, work reviews, tax records, medical and military histories, rap sheets, journals, diaries—all the paper that has defined your life until now, all consumed before your transfixed eyes. This annihilation has a positive side, however, for like the legendary phoenix, we can rise renewed from the ashes of this pyre as our highest Self—the new man or new woman sharing the one gaze with Love and with one another, which after all has always been the dream at the heart of our yearning, the Christ-consciousness that is also Love's vision for the entire cosmos.

> My heart, when love's Sea of a sudden burst into its viewing,
> Leaped headlong in, with "Find me now who may!"
> —Rûmî, *Divâni Shamsi Tabriz*

Returning from the image of this lovely shore to the high desert, however, we will discover that such likewise is the effect of the final push up Mystic Mountain. This is rarified air we breathe. We have reached that altitude where human effort becomes extremely challenging—useless in fact. Parched and weakened as we are from the steepness of our climb and our increased thirst for the Godhead, our only recourse is absolute surrender to the force of this Love, for from this point It alone can lead us to the mountain's hidden springs. Our stance has to become a series of *yes, yes, and yes* as Love continues to transform the old self.

> Empty yourself completely and sit waiting, content with the grace of God, like the chick who tastes nothing and eats nothing but what its mother brings it.
> —Romuald, *Brief Rule for Camaldolese Monks*

Amen, so be it. Whether racing or plodding, we have gone as far as we can through our own activity. From here, Love must be the prime mover. *Love is flowing like a river*, and all we can do is make ourselves available and receptive to Its flow. The plunge into Love is a deep one, as we shall see, and will thoroughly test our courage and resolve. The more completely we immerse ourselves in this stream, however, the safer our course will be and the sooner we will discover our true nature, which is nothing less than that selfsame Love.

Surrendering to Love

> All the activity of man in the works of self-denial has no good in itself, but is only to open an entrance for the one only Good, the light of God, to operate upon us.
> —William Law

In the first two chapters, we looked at surrender as practiced in the active stage of the mystic way, for example surrendering our old attachments and surrendering our time to serve others. We also mentioned surrender as it related to our past and future when we learned to live increasingly in the now. In the context of passive purgation, however, we are faced with letting go of every object, every thought, every belief and every wish we've associated with who we are, offering up the ego to complete annihilation, or rather baring its hollow falsity to unstinting Light. We will be left absolutely destitute to experience poverty in ways we have never imagined.

Unreserved capitulation to the revelation at work within us is the surest way to expose the ego to the Love that is striving mightily to share with us its infinite Being, to the Love that is, in fact, infinitely more eager for us than we are for It. In the words of Sri Ramakrishna,

> As a devotee cannot live without God, so also God cannot live without his devotee. Then the devotee becomes the sweetness, and God its enjoyer. The devotee becomes the lotus, and God the bee. It is the Godhead that has become these two in order to enjoy his own Bliss.

Love can achieve Its purpose in us only with our consent. Johannes Tauler taught, *it asks one thing of us, that It might find the lofty ground with which It endowed man's spirit empty and prepared so that It might accomplish Its eternal work within it*. To achieve this, we must let Love help us transcend all within us that is not divine. As the spirit lifts, the more ballast we jettison, the more the soul *is seized by a powerful longing to be denuded and freed from everything that separates it from God ... and when the denuded ground is touched*, the desire for God *often overflows into flesh and blood and bone*,[33] that is, our *entire being* is absorbed in intense desire for union with the Godhead.

Surrender at this depth is beyond rational comprehension, and also beyond choice now that we have glimpsed Ultimate Reality. Submitting to Love is our only option, which is to say,

---

[33] Johannes Tauler, Sermon "*Surge, Jerusalem ...*," "Rise up Jerusalem and shine forth!"

the small self has no option. Releasing the ego and what it feels it needs becomes the sole order of the day.

To the extent that the small self decreases, the true Self can increase. Insofar as we empty ourselves and transcend the small self, Love rushes to fill the vacancy. Both God and nature abhor a vacuum and when our spirit, the sacred meeting space at the core of our being, is unencumbered, Love *must* act and infuse Itself into us. Our task in this transition from the active to the passive aspects of our journey is to sweep up the remaining rubbish in our hearts and truck it to the dump, offering the cleared space to Love that It might replace the useless debris with a new heart. Matthew Fox summarized, "Letting *go* and letting *be* allow letting *in* to occur."

During this movement of Love, we live as it were on two levels, partly grounded in the Godhead even as we realize that our small self is gradually disappearing, dwindling like *The Incredible Shrinking Woman*. Ideally, we will place that diminishing self more and more at the service of the true Self, as a mortal form through which the Godhead can manifest holiness and compassion. We will continue for a time to look upon the world through human eyes, but eventually they tend to glaze over. All outside tumult blurs to a shimmering backdrop, like heat waves in a desert, and we will see nothing but the holiness of the One Only God enveloping and blessing all existence, God embracing and shining through every scene or person that enters our sight or our consciousness. Then it is that we see all creation, all being, through God's eyes.

Into the Dark

First coffee comes at 5:30 on the late January morning I'm writing this. The quarter moon has already set and except for the brilliance of stars, the hermitage my wife and I share is buried in darkness. The nights have already grown shorter, however. Since the winter solstice we've gained a half hour of daylight in the morning and another half hour in the evening. With midday temperatures in the sixties, the itch of spring already teases our afternoons. And already, I'm missing winter.

We are creatures of the dark. We are conceived and our bodies form in darkness. We protest with all the strength of our newbie lungs when we are pulled into the harsh light of birth. Our vital organs function in the darkness of our shells. Thoughts simmer in the darkness of our minds until we breathe them into daylight. Darkness, even though it has come to represent danger or evil, is our most natural element and, during the winter months of introspection, is the actual condition in which we spend most of our hours.

No wonder the spiritual masters insist that Love can lead us to the Godhead only in obscurity, that we can glimpse divinity in this life only "through a glass darkly." Genesis tells us that creation began with the words *Let there be light*, and until then, we tend to assume, the Godhead existed in primordial darkness. To paraphrase John of the Cross, we might say that to arrive at a place we know not, we must go by a way we know not (see his *Ascent of Mount Carmel*, 1.13). No wonder, then, that our most fundamental inclination when we want to grow is to plunge ourselves in darkness, like plants that in their botanical wisdom root themselves in the rich underground. Courageous surrender, patience and endurance are all now; there is nothing else to do but root ourselves in Love's black soil while It renews Its work of cultivation within us, abiding insofar as possible in simplicity and peace.

All the changes and transformation that occur in the soul from here on can be attributed to the inpouring of Love into the soul and to the form of prayer called *dark contemplation*. As the intellect and will surrender their functions, their need to judge and control and their need for self-preservation, Love will infuse us with inner wisdom, enlightening and purifying our minds, stealthily as it were, with little awareness on our part.

Few of us live in monastic settings where our daily lives are scheduled, with meals, clothing and housing provided, leaving us free to focus on spirituality. We still have to deal with the necessities of life in the world. The good news is that during this time of darkness, as in earlier stages of our pilgrimage, our *functional* minds remain (more or less) intact, allowing us to pay our bills, drive a car or draw up a grocery list. The functional mind is not concerned with ego preservation, but with *process*, recognizing a chore to be done and doing it. The "more or less" part will awaken or confirm our belief in guardian angels, because *something* carries us along with timely reminders or cautions, even when we feel addlepated as we try to attend to detail.

On the mystic way, we have reached the *crux* (literally the cross) of our journey. Through infused contemplation and the suspension of reason we have been led ever so lovingly into the darkness of *unknowing*. We have reached the limits of the intellect and have agreed to surrender to the guidance of Love. We've brought no torch or flashlight with us, prepared to move completely blind through the darkness. We find we are actually eager to submit to the final stripping of all that we thought we were, or willed or possessed and to arrive at that poverty of spirit that will make us irresistible to the Beloved. We enter gladly the cloud of ignorance that shrouds the highest reaches of Mystic Mountain, having abandoned the last recognizable trail, with only trust in Love's benevolence to lead us on. We understand at last that the beginning of wisdom is to know that we do not know.

Dark contemplation, the surrender and death of the ego, the leap into the abyss of poverty and the night of the spirit described in the remainder of this chapter are part and parcel of a single movement with a single goal: to disperse the last vestiges of the small self, of our "self-ishness," so that naught remains but our naked being. The final traces of ego one-by-one must dissipate and the darkness of mind and will must deepen until we arrive at the ground of utter dispossession. Then we can wrap our nakedness in the mantle that has always cloaked the holy ones, that is, in the words of Kierkegaard, *to will one thing*.

Dark contemplation

Before we entered the high desert, we had already experienced several stages of prayer:

- Verbal prayer and devotional prayer of praise
- Cosmic prayer in which we prayed as a universal priesthood

- The prayer of centering recollection, both recollection through our own activity and infused recollection (the prayer of silence, prayer of simplicity or the prayer of quiet)
- Spiritual sleep

In the desert, partially thanks to the discipline we developed earlier, we are led beyond recollection and quiet into still deeper states of contemplation. As characterized in Teresa of Avila's *Interior Castle*, these are:

- The prayer of union
- Ecstatic prayer or rapture, during which we stand outside our senses

As in the infused prayer of quiet, the prayer of union shuts down all thought, including the conscious use of mantras, all physical sensation and any sense of willing anything. We are at rest, suspended in God, with no notion of either the divine attributes or our own. Our focus, if we can call such mindlessness "focus," is on That-Which-Is beyond all imagery, the Nameless, *Is-Ness*, pure Being. We offer God the modest circumstance of our emptied existence. We meet on the level of shared being.

> The journey of the pilgrim is two steps and no more:
> One is the passing out of selfhood,
> and one towards mystical Union with the Friend.
> —Shabistari

This prayer likewise is infused, but now we don't make even that slight mental effort, *the naked reaching out toward God*, the *loving attentiveness* we practiced in the prayer of quiet. We are in a condition of utter absorption, face-to-face with ultimate nothingness—or rather, No-thing meets Itself within our spirits and speaks to Itself face-to-face.

At this point, the contemplation practiced by the mystics of the West begins to resemble Eastern meditation, and particularly the *beginner's mind* of Buddhism. For example, compare this state to Shunryu Suzuki's comment on Zen meditation:

> To go beyond our thinking faculty, it is necessary to have a firm conviction in the emptiness of your mind. ... Actually, emptiness of mind is not even a state of mind, but the original essence of mind that Buddha ... experienced. 'Essence of mind,' 'original mind,' 'original face,' 'Buddha nature,' 'emptiness'—all these words mean the absolute calmness of our mind.[34]

We need to be empty so Love can *speak to our hearts*. Love works in total obscurity within us, lighting the darkness of our minds by Its infusion of divine and purifying understanding, so secretly for the most part that Its movements are hidden even from us who benefit from them. The insights that *do* reach the level of consciousness stir pure astonishment within us. Consider the ecstatic words of Catherine of Genoa:

> When God sees the soul pure as it was in its origins, he tugs at it with a glance, draws it and binds it to himself with a fiery love that by itself could annihilate the immortal soul. In so acting, God so transforms the soul in him that it knows nothing other than God, and he continues to draw it up into his fiery love until he restores it to that pure state from which it first issued.[35]

Prayer at this level is at its root unpretentious. In fact, I use the term "prayer" advisedly when writing of this loftier contemplation. It is rather a pure awareness of *being* with God—and *in* God—while at the same time totally conscious of God *within us*. We hold an unwavering conviction of our single, mutual indwelling and in the face of this awareness have little choice but to forfeit all *methods* of prayer and practice. Instead, we stare in wonder, like thumb-sucking infants, scarcely able to fathom the wondrous change Love has wrought in our hearts.

In the language of Teresa of Avila, we have arrived at *spiritual betrothal*, although not yet the union of *mystical marriage*. Separating the two is the abyss of utter poverty on

---

[34] Shunryu Suzuki, *Zen Mind, Beginner's Mind* (Boston: Shambhala Publications, 1970)
[35] Catherine of Genoa, *Purgation and Purgatory*

whose far side awaits the light-filled nuptial banquet. Not surprisingly, the spirit in this state burns to consummate its relationship with the Beloved.

> Such persons [do] not mind if the operations of their faculties are being lost to them; they should desire rather that this be done quickly so they may not be obstacles to the operation of the infused contemplation God is bestowing so they may ... make room in the spirit for the enkindling and burning of the love that this dark and secret contemplation ... communicates to the soul. For contemplation is nothing else than a secret and peaceful and loving inflow of God, which, if not hampered, fires the soul in the spirit of love.[36]

Ecstasy and rapture

In the highest forms of contemplation, such as the prayer of union (or in spiritual sleep), our spirits can be literally seized, rapt involuntarily and separated from the body. Sometimes this comes about from concentration on a special symbol, such as a crucifix or an icon or a mandala. Completely entranced, we lose all awareness of the world around us and ignore all cues from our bodies and senses. We can remain in this deathlike trance for hours or even days while the body stiffens and turns cold and breathing nearly ceases.

> The soul is thus separated from the body with its power and love and longing. Only the smallest part of life remains to the body which is as it were in a sweet sleep. And [God] clothes it with such garments as are worn in [the] palace [of heaven], and girds it with strength. Then it may ask for what it wills; it will be granted to it.
> —Mechtild of Magdeburg

What one learns during these times generally remains the secret of the person who experiences it. Those who have tried to explain, while they can recall the physical aspects and can even report such bodily changes as renewed health and energy, have never been able to describe the "secret knowledge" imparted to them by God. They know they have been in direct contact and

---

[36] John of the Cross, *The Dark Night*, 1.10.6

spoken with Ultimate Being, they know that the memory of this meeting will remain with them forever, but the *message* received in ecstasy is inexplicable.

Needless to say, ecstasy is sweet and can be a good thing if it evolves from the loftiest states of contemplation. It requires great courage to go through such experiences, however, for they can literally be life threatening. The ecstatic can die if the spirit permanently leaves the body as it shuts down physically, or in some cases from the sheer intensity of their fervor and incredible joy. An Eastern belief is that a *golden cord* or *golden thread* connects body and spirit during these flights—a cord not to be broken through interruption or disturbance, as the spirit may not be able to scramble back to the body. It leaves the body and travels elsewhere during this "sleep." If a person is startled, or the cord is somehow severed while in this state, he or she may not survive.

In her description of the sixth dwelling of the *Interior Castle* and in Chapter 20 of her *Life*, Teresa of Avila catalogs numerous extraordinary experiences such as voices and visions and levitation, to which we in modern parlance might add astral projection, out-of-body experiences, extrasensory perception, or "gifts of the Spirit" like prophesy and speaking in tongues.

Because these happenings can be so entrancing, both literally and figuratively, spiritual teachers generally warn against provoking or lingering over them. Chogyam Trungpa Rinpoche, for example, sees this as a realm of *spiritual materialism* and a way the ego can regain a foothold within us. These days we can even attend workshops that will teach us how to levitate and presumably make us the life of the next party we go to. Thomas Merton warned against *delusions* that *aim to establish the ego in spiritual glory*, and Alice Bailey dismissed them as *glamours*. Teresa herself allowed that many ecstasies experienced by her nuns were but *raptures of feminine weakness*. Dom Augustine Baker summed up all these misgivings:

> Ecstasies that do not produce considerable profit either to the persons themselves or to others deserve to be suspected, and when any marks of their approaching are

perceived, the persons ought to divert their minds some other way.[37]

We are still short of the summit of Mystic Mountain. This near to our goal, we need not allow parlor tricks and ego infiltration to distract us.

The death of ego

What we hope to experience in blind surrender to Love is the final demise of the ego and its rebirth as the true Self, the spouse worthy of the Beloved. We have long since conceded that we can make no progress with ego as the basis of advancement. Egoic *death* is another way of saying that we must rid ourselves once for all and absolutely of that primal dualism that would have us believe we are separate from others and from the Godhead. We *must* release this belief at our physical death, of course, but as contemplatives we strive to practice ultimate emptiness ahead of time. It is the essence of the mystic way, and a rehearsal for the final, inevitable, separation of body and spirit.

We must die to any activities that might wound us spiritually. This is another understanding of the expression, *dead to the world*, dead to that former mentality. We're not asleep in this *transitus* of the ego, however, but rather are fully alert and conscious. We release our nonspiritual interests and ambitions by choice, responding only to Love's urgings. Our sole abiding wish is to live in Love alone, just as Love lives in us, and to obey Its dictates.

Since the beginning, Love has been at work, redefining our human makeup—our mind, with its memories and imagination, our will, our psyche, soul and spirit. These aspects of our human nature are neither pure enough nor strong enough nor capable of receiving supernatural gifts until the old self disappears. This is why Love must purge them and lead them into increasing darkness. The mind cannot grasp the nature of the Godhead, and so must proceed in the blindness of unknowing. The will is bereft of its usual, tangible love objects and is left instead to love an invisible and unfathomable

---

[37] Augustine Baker, *Holy Wisdom*, (1850) Treatise 3.4.3

Entity, straining its normal feelings of affection. Love, as it happens, is reinterpreted in this process. It now means doing God's will as we understand it, often totally devoid of warm feeling. The imagination is similarly lost, for it can form no picture of the Infinite, and in fact the more it tries to visualize Divinity, the further it moves away from Its Being.

To add to the confusion, we may at times feel we know something of the Godhead in this dark way, but without love; at other times it might seem that we love passionately while knowing nothing. Perhaps this is a way to say we are drawn alternately to the negative and positive mystic ways. And all the while we continue to inhabit our mortality, where the physical and nonphysical intersect and we seldom know for certain what is really happening with us. For example, a friend had his thyroid removed. Over the next decades, various doctors prescribed versions of thyroxin for him in a range of strengths. At the highest dosage he watched with bemusement while the full spectrum of human emotion swung through him like a roller coaster on overdrive. At the lowest dosage his wife complained that he never showed any passion, up or down.

When I was a beginning meditator in my early thirties, I quieted my mind enough to become aware of a steady hum within my head. Like a small dynamo, it purred constantly at an unvarying and curiously reassuring pitch. It has stayed with me for the last 40 years, no matter where I lived—by the ocean, on mountainsides, in the city or country. At first I thought I had tapped perhaps into the pure energy vibrating through all creation, however one names that life-power, or at least into the bioenergetic fields or low-frequency electromagnetic radiation that surround and interpenetrate us. The Force was with me. Or perhaps I had attended one too many rock concerts.

A decade or so later, I read of HCE, hyper cerebral electrolysis, and opined that I actually might be listening to brain activity. I never consulted a doctor because I found it a pleasant, reliable and consistent pattern in an otherwise inconsistent world. Now in my seventies, I find I can get "inside the sound" at will to a place of utter silence, figuring that any brain activity must cease completely in that space. Someday I may discover that my initial intuition of the hum as the vibration of pure energy, the divine *Hu*, was correct and that this universal energy is none other than me (and you).

My wife, while visiting a convent in the Marches of Italy, whiffed an odor that made her think of oil that might have been used in medieval times as furniture polish. The scent still comes to her in meditation, but her doctor has dismissed it as an olfactory hallucination. And what of that burning in the heart reported by numerous mystics? Is it the refinement of Love, Kali energy, or merely heartburn? Well, certainly it is a heart aflame, whatever its source. The physical sensation of various chakras spinning wildly, most often at the heart center, is common also. The body, apparently, will insist that it be included in this journey we have undertaken.

Surrendering the ego is the basic principle of self-emptying, of being weaned from all that is not God. The first great commandment of the Torah is to love God above all else, with all our heart and mind and strength, and this we can do only in the absence of everything that is not of God.

Love, when it inflames the spirit, removes us from the small self. Our past proclivities hold no more appeal for us, although they may have been powerful motivators in their day. This is the freedom mystics celebrate with great joy. The gift of Love is the gift of emptiness and emancipation from all that once entangled us. It is also a gift we willingly return. The gift springs from That-Which-Is and once we have emptied our own spirit and are delivered of ego, of all dualism and our ancient baggage, we can enter the Source of the gift, the nakedness of the Godhead, offering to It the nakedness of our own being. Meister Eckhart said, when speaking of dualism, that

> The spirit has to go beyond all quantity and break through all diversity. Then it will be broken through by God. Quite the same way, however, as God breaks through me, I shall break through him in return![38]

---

[38] Meister Eckhart, Sermon *Convescens praecepit eis* ..., ("Eating with them, he instructed them not to leave Jerusalem")

We can, moreover, view Love's work within us as a *remembering*, a *wakening* of our true memory of who we are. Baal Shem Tov, the founder of the Hasidic movement, instructed his followers, *in remembrance resides the secret of redemption.* As we have been constantly reminded in our reading and by other teachers, we need only remember that we are *already* "redeemed," that we and That-Which-Is are *already* intimately joined, that It *already is* our own deepest Being. That we don't remember we can attribute to the smoke screens raised by our human condition and the imperatives of survival during our unaware years. We share a world mired in dualism, the *quantity and diversity* deplored by Meister Eckhart, and this is why Love must lead us into the emptiness and pure unity of the high desert where our spirit can rise through ever higher levels of integration into the Godhead.

Through unstinting surrender, our former (and sometimes current) reluctance and spiritual foot-dragging are transfigured into a tool for resisting the tenacity of our clinging egos. We finally arrive at a place where we acknowledge that outside God we are nothing, that in God we are everything. In our growing homesickness our lone question becomes: when will I arrive at spiritual marriage? When will the Beloved consummate my longing for union? Please note that the question is no longer "What can *I do* to make this happen?"

Once more I would offer a word of caution about the inner working of Love, or rather repeat the earlier call to patience. We can find ourselves submersed in the experiences of illumination, dark contemplation, and subsequent purgation for a seeming eternity. Having emerged from the lower slopes where we actively struggled up Mystic Mountain, having advanced beyond the state of *novice* seekers, which in itself may have required years or decades, we typically spend more years in what spiritual writers call the condition of *proficients.* We are still short of the summit, the realm of *perfected masters,* but at least we know now that Love is leading us in that direction.

A prayer I learned in childhood, based on the Wisdom Books and Psalm 104, asks specifically for the help of Spirit:

> Come Holy Spirit,
> enlighten our minds.
> Enkindle in our hearts the fire of your love.
> Send forth your Spirit
> And we shall be (re)created,
> And you shall renew the face of the earth.

Yes, this is still a prayer of petition, the ego asking Spirit for what it thinks it needs, and a typical prayer of institutional religion. However, this is in fact what Love wishes to give us. It is God praying through us, God asking God to give God what It already is. The twin flames of inner light and divine Love that we ask for in the prayer will be most useful in the state of unknowing.

The interior work of Love during this phase is what John of the Cross called the dark nights of the sensual and spiritual parts of the soul. On the path up Mystic Mountain, we have willingly allowed Love to draw us into these nights in pursuit of the Godhead who dwells in darkness. We come eventually to the threshold of an unbridgeable fissure, a seemingly fathomless chasm, and have no other means to reach the far side and resume our ascent than to step off the edge and sink into its dusky profundity. The darkness and fog at this height makes the leap into the abyss all the more terrifying, for we are stepping off into a cloudbank—a leap of faith and hope, of "falling upward" as Richard Rohr might characterize it. So it is on this paradoxical pilgrimage that we speak of tumbling and rising as features of the same path.

As we take this plunge and ego-consciousness is released in the free-fall, we will discover a further paradox. We've been thinking that we had to reach the "other side" of the chasm, but once we simply *are*, we will realize that the chasm never had "sides." We have not yet arrived in this realization, however, and so we take the dreaded next step, quaking like a bound prisoner forced to walk the plank that will plunge him into the ocean's abyss.

Bede Griffiths, distilled all this sense of mystic death and the leap into darkness when he wrote of contemplation, "It feels like death and is a sort of dying. It is encountering the darkness, the abyss, the void. It is facing nothingness or, as the

English Benedictine mystic Augustine Baker said, *it is the union of the nothing with the Nothing.*"[39]

The abyss of poverty

> The Path of Love is like a Bridge of Hair
> across a Chasm of Fire
> —Early-Christian mystic

> The abysmal Waylessness of God is so dark and so unconditioned that it swallows up in itself every divine way and activity ... and brings about a divine fruition in the abyss of the Ineffable. And here there is a ... melting and dying into the Essential Nudity, where all the divine names, and all conditions, and all the living images which are reflected in the mirror of divine truth, lapse in the Onefold and Ineffable, in waylessness and without reason.[40]

Thus we teeter on the brink of a sheer precipice, wobbling like the setting sun as it tries to balance on the ocean's rim, resisting earth's rotation away from the skyline. There are those who *must* look over the edge down into the darkness and those who *cannot*. Those who do, often find themselves staring into the heart of breakage and potential insanity. Our only option, however, should we choose to continue this journey, is to leap like mindless madmen into the unknown. We must abandon the soul's comfort zone in the name of Love, like fledglings that will never learn to fly unless they launch themselves off the edge of their nest. The question is, will we sprout wings like eagles (Isaiah 40:31), or be borne up by God's angels lest we dash our foot against a stone (Psalm 91), or have we jumped unwittingly into the yawning maw of mental meltdown, there to twist for the rest of our days in spasms of despair?

Plunging off the edge without a parachute is what spiritual writers of the 1960s and 1970s were fond of calling "crazy wisdom," for it defies sanity and logic. Think about it! We hover

---

[39] Bede Griffiths, *The Inner Directions Journal*, (Inner Directions Foundation), Summer, 1996
[40] Jan van Ruysbroeck, *Op. Cit.*, 3.4

on the threshold of a nose-dive into No-thing-ness, letting go of every fastener that has held us together until now, every belief system and concept of the finite or the infinite, every familiar mooring, every sense of belonging to anything outside, of others' expectations of us, everything we associate with who we've been and are or could be, our feelings, our perceptions, every link to the time and places through which we familiarly move. This surrender also includes the kit and caboodle of our observable universe and even our *consciousness* of this cosmic palette. Absolutely nuts!

The free-fall can be paralyzing, too, for the illusory ego is ever anxious to prove it is still meaningful and will wrestle us to the bottom, insisting all the way down that we are fools to abandon our precious selves. The plummet is terrifying as well in its obscurity and infinite vastness, in its total lack of handholds or ledges where we might temporarily rest, in its sheer illogic—and in its lack of any guarantee that someone will be there to catch us. Yet this last fear becomes our sole hope. We can overcome the terror only by reminding ourselves to trust in the goodness of Divinity, by repeating that we have chosen wisely and by renewing our conviction that Love will lead us always by exactly the best course. Our constant prayer: *De profundis clamavi ad te, Domine*; *out of the depths I have cried to you, O Lord.*

Regina Sara Ryan described in detail the dread that seized her when she realized that she had come to this precipice and understood also the full magnitude of the leap. The world she currently inhabited would fragment forever should her surrender at that moment be absolute.

> Walking along a hillside nearby the house in which I stayed, as I repeated a mantra and fingered my prayer beads, I was stopped in mid-step by awareness that I was literally approaching the edge of the known universe. *My known universe*! There was no vision. There were no lights. There were certainly no voices of guidance or prophecy. But there was an interior *knowing* that surrender as I had always prayed for it was right there in front of me. I was on the edge of the abyss of myself, and about to step off

into nothingness, if only I put my foot down to complete that awesome step. *Freeze!*[41]

And there is that moment when we freeze and take stock of all that we've been and might yet be in our known world, and of what we will abandon if we continue. Fight and flight are not the only reactions to "danger." Think of the deer in the headlights, or a small animal immobilized as a hawk swoops in. The invitation to leap might not be as clear for us as it was for Regina, but the fear should be. Realistically, the timing might not be right for us at this instant. We might not be ready to dive headlong into the fire of Love, the conflagration that will burn away the last residue of all that we have been until now. A further, distinct message came to Regina, that It is not we who surrender, but Love that "surrenders us" at the perfect moment—at Its pace and timing—for It is now in charge of this journey.

Her comment that she stared down into the abyss of *herself* is also intriguing, for this void is nothing less than the depths of our own minds and wills. It is a cavernous mine gleaming with useless "treasures" that Love must plumb, root out and consume on Its bonfire so that It might refill that immensity, making of it a reservoir of boundless affection, analogous perhaps to the salt caves that hold America's strategic oil reserves. For us pilgrims, what is *strategic* is that we let Love lead us into and through the deepest recesses of this cavern, the only place we can hope to rediscover our rudimentary Self. The journey is both awful and awesome and may feel at times like Dante's descent through the rings of hell. *Deep is calling unto Deep* (Psalm 42).

Blessed are the poor in spirit

The chasm of ultimate surrender may seem unfathomable as we stare into the numberless layers of our own being, but it is, in fact, not bottomless. We reach its deepest layer through radical poverty, the nearly inconceivable nakedness Meister Eckhart described in his sermon *Beati pauperes spiritu* ("Blessed are the Poor in Spirit"). Those who know such poverty, said the Meister, *will nothing, know nothing, and have*

---

[41] Regina Sara Ryan, *Op. Cit.*, pp. 128-9.

nothing. (John of the Cross scribbled on his map of Mount Carmel, that the way to God is *nada, nada, nada, nada, nada, nada, nada*—seven times *nothing.*)

In his sermon Meister Eckhart distinguished between the commonplace, exterior notion of poverty, even pious poverty, and sheer, inner poverty of spirit. (Note in the following quotations, as in earlier comments from Meister Eckhart, "God" refers to That-Which-Is; "god" refers to Divinity as filtered through human imagination, god as we have created "him.")

The usual notion of *poverty of will* is that we submit our wants to God's will as part of our surrender and penitential exercises, and that we accept without complaint whatever God sends our way. This, Meister Eckhart said, leaves us clinging to the selfish "I," for the wish to please God is still *our* will:

> For human beings to possess true poverty, [they] must be as free of [their] created will as they were when they did not exist. ... As long as you have a will, even the will to fulfill God's will, and as long as you have the desire for eternity and for God, to this very extent you are not properly poor. ...

Like Meister Eckhart, William Law saw the self-centered will as the primary obstacle to union with God. The basic question arises, are we still the hub of our lives? Does our universe, like the pre-Copernican model of the cosmos, still radiate from and revolve around our small self? *Nothing has separated us from God but our own will,* Law said, *or rather our own will is our separation from God. All the disorder and corruption and malady of our nature lies in a certain fixedness of our will, and imagination and desire, wherein we live to ourselves, are our own center and circumference, act wholly from ourselves.* The whole point of surrendering to the abyss, he adds, is that *the deepest root of all selfishness, as well spiritual as natural, is to be plucked up and torn from us ... to make that final surrender which is the price of final peace.*[42]

---

[42] William Law, "Christian Regeneration"

Detachment in this instance includes releasing even the notion of our potential for God-realization. As Thomas Merton wrote, *As soon as there is "someone there" to have a transcendent experience, "the experience" is falsified and indeed becomes impossible.*

Meister Eckhart expanded on his point by reminding his congregation of their pre-creation origin in Being, in the perfection that preceded their birth into imperfect humanity.

When I still stood in my first cause, there I had no god and was cause of myself. There I willed nothing. I desired nothing, for I was a pure being and a knower of myself in delight of the truth. There I willed myself and nothing else. What I willed, that I was; and what I was, that I willed. There I stood, free of god and of all things. But when I took leave from this state of free will and received my created being, then I had a god. Indeed, before creatures were, [the Godhead] was not yet "god;" rather he was what he was. But when creatures came to be and when they received their created being, then God was no longer God in himself; rather he was god in creatures.

He made the same point about *poverty of knowledge* as he did about *poverty of will*. People should stand empty, as free of knowledge as when they were not yet created.

Whoever achieves this poverty must so live that *they not even know themselves to live* [emphasis mine], either for oneself or for truth or for God ... letting God accomplish whatever God wills. ... People should keep themselves free and void so that they neither understand nor know that God works in them.

When he spoke of *having nothing*, he again distinguished between having (or not having) material possessions, of external poverty (which mattered not so long as one didn't cling to these things), versus true poverty of spirit:

If people stand free of all things, of all creatures, of god and of themselves, but if it still happens that God can find a place for acting in them, then we say: So long as that is so, these persons are not poor in the strictest poverty. For God does not desire that people reserve a place for him to work in. Rather, true poverty of spirit consists in keeping oneself so free of god and of all one's works that if God wants to act in the soul, God himself must *be* the place in which he acts. ... Where people reserve some place in themselves, they preserve distinction. This is why I pray God to rid me of god.

For Meister Eckhart, the goal of radical poverty is the same as that of sitting zazen, to return to that state in which we existed before we entered time—original, empty mind. In the *Gospel of the Blessed Companion*, Jesus' observation that we must become like little children to enter the kingdom of heaven is translated in one redaction, *unless you become like babies.* Even to know that we know God is distressing to Meister Eckhart: *If this (blessedness) suffices for other persons, let them keep it for themselves, but let it be spared for me!* He would say that true blessedness is simply to *be* That-Which-Is. *The soul knows nothing about knowledge or love or anything else. It wishes to be completely at rest and exclusively in God's Being.*[43]

Once again, this denuded ground of being is best arrived at in the *now*, when we sit immersed in Divinity, in the deeps of contemplation. Just *now*, in this perfect instant, you can set down this book, settle into the divine presence, and let go of all thoughts so that you *know* nothing, let go of all desires and even longing for God so that you *will* nothing, and release all attachments to any place or object so that you *have* nothing. This is the end of all our contemplation.

When we are totally poor, absolutely empty of self, then God *is* that place where It wants to act. When we have surrendered everything to That-Which-Is, the Beloved rushes to caress us in our profound nakedness. Love lights the abyss of our passive mind and soul as with innumerable torches and the deep, in return, reflects this radiance back to its Source. We offer to the Godhead, along with unwavering surrender, the gifts of Light and Love with which It fills our emptiness.

---

[43] Meister Eckhart, Treatise, Vom edlen Menschen, ("Concerning the Aristocrat")

We said earlier that this leap into the abyss is a dry run, or undressed rehearsal, for death. As contemplatives, we have no fear of death's eternal silence for we know that a beneficent tenderness indwells that void. Resting in God, we can anticipate in the time-dimension the gentle welcome that awaits us in the stillness beyond time. Even in this lifetime, we will be tugged often to the shore of that ocean where mortality ends and glorified life begins, drawn by a combination of eagerness to be with the Beloved, by curiosity, by homesickness. We know, however, that for now we must follow as well as we can the advice of the Flemish mystic:

> This is that wayless [form of] being which all interior spirits have chosen above all other things. This is the dark silence in which all lovers lose themselves. But if we would prepare ourselves for it, ... we should strip ourselves of all but our very bodies, and should flee forth into the wild Sea, whence no created thing can draw us back again.
> —Jan van Ruysbroeck

It is with reluctance, then, that we turn back to finish the work assigned us on this planet, a delay that in itself is a major cause of the powerful suffering we now experience. We have come to accept not only *what* our small self is, but *that* it is. We know that we must continue to exist in human form for the unknown and, to our yearning hearts, interminable span of months or years yet demanded of us.

The dark nights

We speak here of two nights, *the dark night of the senses*, which completes the work of detachment begun in the forest, and *the dark night of spirit*. They are linked and become one operation of Love because within our human makeup, body and mind, soul and spirit, are intrinsically joined.

In the dark night of the senses, Love finished the purgation begun at the mountain's base during our active practice. We haven't the capacity to finish this work alone, which is less a purging at this point than a bridling of sensual distractions and desires. The latter lose their customary appeal through sheer aridity. In the dry heat of the desert, the senses are calmed and placed as it were in a state of suspended animation, awaiting the sublimation that occurs in the night of the spirit. The senses, after all, take their marching orders from the reactions of the mind and soul to their constant stimulation, and until the latter achieve the harmony of pure intention, the senses can only flounder.

The dark night of the spirit—another name for crossing the desert, for the Zen sickness of the East and the despair described in the *Sickness unto Death* of Søren Kierkegaard—prepares the highest aspect of our being so that the spiritual betrothal experienced during the prayer of union can be consummated in mystical marriage. The lower and higher aspects of the soul are stripped together in dark contemplation and by our free-fall into the radical abandonment, poverty and emptiness of the abyss.

> I see my soul alienated from all spiritual things that could give it solace and joy. It has no taste for the things of the intellect, will or memory, and in no manner tends more to one thing than to another. Quite still and in a state of siege, the *me* within finds itself gradually stripped of all those things that in spiritual or bodily form gave it some comfort; and once the last of them has been removed, the soul, understanding that they were at best supportive, turns its back on them completely.[44]

Suffering in darkness

> I am the one he has driven and forced to walk in darkness and without any light. ... He has walled me about so I cannot escape. He has put heavy chains on me, and when I call and cry for help, he shuts out my prayer. He has blocked my ways with hewn stones; he has obstructed my paths.
> —Lamentations, 3:1-2, 7-9

The incredible wrenching of the spirit in this crossing from illumination to union might be likened to the pangs of childbirth, the suffering necessary to birth cosmic consciousness within us. As Meister Eckhart asked in a Christmas sermon, *What does it avail me if this birth takes*

---

[44] Catherine of Genoa, *Purgation and Purgatory*

place unceasingly and yet does not take place within me? And as with childbirth, we cannot change our minds back once the contractions begin.

> We have conceived and been born in the pains of labor
> and have brought for the spirit of salvation.
> —Isaiah 26:17-18

Nothing in our training has prepared us for this happening, poles apart from our lifelong understanding of the world. There is a sense of abnormality in our workaday universe because our spirits have been introduced in human form to experiences more suited to other dimensions. We earthlings, no matter how spiritual we strive to be, can't help but agonize in this utter disruption and dislocation of our natural state.

Given our increasingly limited understanding of this passage through unknowing, we wonder what is actually happening to us. We can react both physically and spiritually to the dark night but, with bodily symptoms we have to wonder whether there is a medical basis for the changes we feel or whether they are symptoms of this movement of Love. This is the situation in which Catherine of Genoa found herself, slowly dying it seemed, but for no fathomable reason. Her doctors finally gave up trying to diagnose her condition, stating that her symptoms were "supernatural" and beyond treatment.

We may become lethargic emotionally, mentally and physically, prone to boredom and spiritual fatigue in our practices. Under another name, this is the *aridity* common to the high desert. We feel hollow. The body is an empty husk. No one is home. The mind no longer works. The small self approaches the terminus of no-self. Acutely aware of the temporary nature of our bodies, of our thoughts, our histories, and anything related to us, we reach a condition where we feel we are sliding into nothingness. Kathleen Dowling Singh wrote of the physical death that parallels this spiritual night, *it is not so much that we renounce the world in the course of dying—the world simply slips away. The sense of self slips away. The old structures of ego identity are seen to have no reality whatsoever, can no more be held onto than can a billow of smoke.*[45]

At other times, we may find our mind overwhelmed with impulses we thought we had long since overcome, as though we were back at the trailhead of the forest path. All the long-dormant lower urges we thought we had purified invade the surface and, once again, all we can do is recognize and accept these shadows as part of our total being and offer them to Love for healing. Recall the earlier quotation from Ken Wilber pointing out how we, as humans, can be highly evolved in some areas of our development, while at the same time we may exhibit poor or pathological behavior in other areas. At no step of the way will we be past the need for divine aid and mercy.

When students of Rabbi Pinhas worried that the "Evil Urge" was pursuing them, he replied: *Don't worry. You have not gotten high enough for it to pursue you. For the time being you are still pursuing it.* Whether we are the pursuing it or it is pursuing us, the need for vigilance will always be a given.

We may also experience the very opposite of the lassitude mentioned above. A Hindu might think of this as a surge of Kali energy. It can erupt in bursts of constructive creativity and at other times in unexpected, destructive *out*bursts against others. A medieval Christian mystic would likely see the latter as a last-gasp attempt of the devil to ensnare the soul, and even a "saint" as advanced as Teresa of Avila blamed Satan for the "bad temper" that made her want to bite off people's heads. And so the battle rages, although in our weakened condition we may feel less equipped to wage it. Surrender, surrender, surrender to Love and the strength It provides.

> My healing comes from … the shadow. I dip down into that muck again and again and then am flooded with its healing energy. … First I feel the despair, but I deny it for a few days; then its tugs become more insistent in proportion to my resistance; finally it overwhelms me and pulls me down, kicking and screaming all the way. It's clear I am caught, so at last I give up. … Immediately the

---

[45] Kathleen Dowling Singh, *Op. Cit.*, p. 199

release begins: first peace and then the flood of vitality and healing energy.

—Darlene Cohn

And so we must be ever on guard. Although we've climbed a long way from the base of Mystic Mountain through years of worthy effort and practice and now are experiencing the transfiguring work of Love, so long as we remain in the human condition, we can slide back down the path and suffer serious tumbles. The media overwhelm us with stories of preachers lamenting tearfully from their pulpits, "I have sinned," of pedophile priests and scout masters, of gurus and counselors exploiting the fragility of the troubled men and women who come to them for help. When those among us who seemingly have committed their lives to religion and spirituality, or have established themselves as guides and healers, fall so far from Grace, they put us on notice that we need to immerse ourselves constantly in the mercy of divine Love. As I wrote in an earlier chapter, we will find ourselves *shadowboxing* right up to our dying breaths.

The spiritual side is where we suffer most during this passage. We may experience a strong sense of our unworthiness as a result of the self-knowledge and the understanding of God that we have gained along the way, tumbling into prolonged depression as we are forced to admit to ourselves how distant we still remain from the Godhead. Self-recognition in highly refined by now, and the dust motes we wouldn't have noticed in younger years now distract and burden us. The vision of our imperfection, of our warts and tumors, becomes glaringly vivid, and we feel helpless to escape our sense of shame and worthlessness. The lucid image we hold of our spiritual hideousness is in stark contrast to the vision of God's grandeur. Even as we desire the pure beauty that is God, we feel forever unworthy to abide in that presence.

As with a crown of thorns or the ongoing pain of a wound, our only recourse is to endure the suffering second-by-second. *I can bear the ache for this present instant. I can bear the ache in this next instant ...*

Related to this last, another form of spiritual anguish, especially among those focused on a *personal* relationship with

God, is the conviction that we have been totally abandoned by the Beloved for whom we now have an unquenchable desire. Its presence seems to have deserted us and, we feel, deservedly so. Comparing this sense of rejection to a human betrothal, it is as if the prospective bride or groom has suddenly vanished with no explanation, no longer shows up at the usual meeting place, makes no contact, sends no message as to when (or whether) she or he might return.

The difference here is the degree of intensity. The hiddenness of the Beloved during this apparent desertion is not a case of playing hide-and-seek behind a veil. No, it is agony! It makes us want to scream along with Jesus, *Eli, Eli, lama sabacthani. My God, my God, why have you forsaken me*? This is the most poignant torture we suffer during the dark night of the spirit, experienced in proportion to the vehemence of our longing. Love has totally engulfed our hearts. We die a thousand times over for each day that we must endure this separation from the Beloved and some agonized souls feel they might literally die from sheer anguish. Approaching emptiness as a Zen Buddhist, disappearing into the void devoid of personality, would seem to be a definite plus at this juncture.

Those suffering through this sense of desertion may find some comfort in this story of the Baal Shem Tov:

> A disciple asked the Baal Shem: "Why is that one who clings to God and knows he is close to him sometimes experiences a sense of interruption and remoteness?"
>
> The Baal Shem explained: "When a father sets out to teach his little son to walk, he stands in front of him and holds his two hands on either side of the child so that he cannot fall, and the boy goes toward his father between the father's hands. But the moment he is close to his father, he moves away a little and holds his hands farther apart, and he does this over and over so that the child may learn to walk."[46]

---

[46] Martin Buber, *Tales of the Hasidim*, (New York: Schocken Books, 1947), p. 65

Another potential source of pain during this time is awareness not only of our alienation from God, but also from our fellow beings. We can easily isolate ourselves on the spiritual path, allow all sorts of relationships to fall away, withdraw more and more from human contact. Sudden awakening to our disconnection from others can become one more source of upset during this time of transition. How can we grow in patience if no one is around to annoy us? How can we practice compassion separated from suffering humanity? Counsel, likewise, is hard to find, for few spiritual directors and teachers have actually experienced and emerged from this dark passage. We may never in our lives feel so alone and cut off from the world as we do at this time.

This particular angst is curable, although given our extreme fragility during the dark nights and the shutdown of our normal capabilities, this might be an awkward time to be reaching out. We'll return to this issue, however, in the next chapter.

Needless to say, the dark nights, like the contemplative life in general, are not for the faint of heart, whether we endure them in a cloister or as closet contemplatives embedded in the mass of humanity. Facing down the despair and dread felt by the ego as it goes through psychic death requires heroic courage. Such courage Love also provides, often through external or interior trials such as misunderstanding from others, fear of deception in our spiritual quest, being yanked unwillingly from our comfort zone (a recluse forced into public life, a prominent figure forced into the background) and other forms of involuntary *agere contra*. All the conditions of this state can lead to oppression of the spirit, and the worst of these is the sense that God has abandoned us.

My sister-in-law, in the final stages of her cancer, told my wife that God had given her this simple message: "Be still and wait." Like the "suffering servant" foretold by Isaiah, like a Mohandas Gandhi or Etty Hillesum, we overcome suffering by *bearing*. The character of this acceptance also changes during the desert crossing because we are nearer our goal. Did I mention that we now shoulder affliction *eagerly*, run to embrace it when we see it on the way, because we understand that it is preparing us for mystical union with the Beloved? We suffer gladly, because we know that we are being "recreated" by the operation of Love. And in fact, spiritual favors are granted soon after we have endured these tribulations of spirit. This is why saints of every tradition revel in their woundedness and can say with Julian of Norwich that our *dearworthy sufferings* are our glory.

A hopeful thought for those who believe they are presently struggling through this horrific transition (although we can never be sure where we stand on the mystic path): Love purifies us more or less based on our commitment to the journey—that is, how much purgation we are willing to take on—and how much purgation we are *able* to take on—which It knows far better than we. If we find ourselves in the extreme purification of the dark nights, it is a sign that Love wants to lead us to the highest union of which humanity is capable. The severe emptiness of this passage may feel like a cause for tears, but in truth, it is but an (admittedly severe) preparation for the next breakthrough. The sense that *I am not* resulting from this final stripping of the ego leads to the ultimate, shared *I AM*. At last we will have bridged the primal dualism, the sense that we are separate from God. In this union the small self is finally dethroned and replaced by the higher Self as we arrive at the source of our being. Love ingrained with "self-ishness" is disenfranchised. Pure Love assumes its place.

> Once stripped of all its imperfections, the soul rests in God, with no characteristics of its own, since its purification is the stripping away of the lower self in us. Our being is then God.
>
> —Catherine of Genoa

The ferryman punted them dexterously out from shore. Suddenly they saw a body in the water, drifting rapidly downstream. Tripitaka stared at it in consternation. Monkey laughed. "Don't be frightened, Master," he said. "That's you." And Pigsy said, "It's you, it's you." Sandy clapped his hands. "It's you, it's you," he cried. The ferryman too joined in the chorus. "*There you go!*" he cried. "My best congratulations."

—Wu Ch'êng-ên, *Monkey*

Chapter 4. Falling in Love with Love

> ... and blue-bleak embers, ah my dear,
> Fall, gall themselves, and gash gold-vermillion.
> —Gerard Manley Hopkins, "The Windhover"

Emerging from the cloud of unknowing, having survived the thorough debridement of the high desert, we break into brilliant sunshine once more. Spent and utterly helpless though we may feel following this daunting leg of the journey, we happily surrender to the sweep of Love that now carries us to the very summit of Mystic Mountain. We have passed through *extinction* (which is the meaning of *nirvana*) into the state of no-self. Nothing but God now attaches to us. This is the stage of union in Christian mysticism, Zen *satori*, the Supreme Identity of Islam.

When our Godlike spirits merge with Spirit, we pass beyond all human emotion and understanding into pure being. In fact, "we" no longer exist; only Love *is* in all its formlessness and forms. The simple recognition of our Being, even as we remain totally human, puts our existence, as well as the existence of all of creation, into a celestial perspective.

> The monk may look to the past and indeed he may appear to live in the past, but he knows a secret: as Christ is the same today and yesterday and yea, even tomorrow, so is he. He never feels irrelevant because whatever happens, however infinitesimal he is, wherever he is, he knows that without him, creation would not be creation. He is important to the world simply because he is, in the same way that the earth is good simply because it is.[47]

When we first became conscious of Oneness with the Godhead during our time of illumination, there was still a part of us that had the thought, *God and I are One*. The difference between that experience and this merger at the summit is that we don't recognize oneness as a joining of Spirit with our spirits, or as Love pouring into us. Rather, the witness—the

---

[47] Richard John Friedlander, *Paradise Besieged*, (Berkeley: Flying High Press, 2009), p. 190

observer—the observed, and the act of observing fuse. Thought does not even try to comprehend it. In Meister Eckhart's words, there is but *one seeing, one knowing and one loving*. There is only Being, a seamless sphere that enfolds us and, along with us, the entire cosmos. There is *only* Oneness, no-thing here but God. There is no intermediary, no other, no sense of inner or outer, no place *anywhere* but God, no anywhere but *here*. There is no awareness or even the *notion of another*. Any thought, any word, trying to define this union, any attempt to deconstruct this ineffable experience, would introduce separation into it.

The death of the self, its reduction to no-self, has led to rebirth into the life of the Godhead. Love is our new life, the green shoot sprouting from the dark nights' volcanic ash. Our awareness has moved from the details of multiplicity to the nondual vastness of the Absolute, into Buddhahood, *theosis*, Christ- or Cosmic-Consciousness. The crown chakra is spinning like a dervish. We are no longer self-centered, that is, centered in the small self, but rather, our spirits are anchored in God, the deepest center of us and the universe—which is to say we have become Self-centered. The original dualism, the belief that we were from God, has dissolved in Union. We no longer live or act of ourselves. Rather, God lives and acts through us.

The desert father, Evagrius of Pontus, remarked that we know we have reached our destination spiritually when *the spirit begins to see its own light*. In Hindu spirituality, concentration on *the lotus of the heart* also leads to an experience of pure light. In both cases, this light signals that we have met our true Self. Eavesdrop for a moment on one who emerged from darkness and arrived bedazzled by blinding sunlight at the summit:

> The simple ground of our Eternal Image ever remains in ... waylessness, but the brightness without limit which streams forth from it reveals ... the hiddenness of God. And all those who are raised up above their created being into a God-seeing life are one with ... that brightness itself, and they see, feel, and find, even by means of this Divine Light, that, as regards their uncreated essence, they are that same ground from which the brightness without limit

shines forth in the Divine way. ... By means of this inborn light they are transfigured, and made one with that same light through which they see and which they see. And thus the God-seeing follow after their Eternal Image ... and they behold God and all things without distinction, in a simple seeing, in the Divine brightness.[48]

In an earlier chapter we quoted Meister Eckhart who said that God not only breaks through into our spirits, but that we also break through into God. He further described how we offer our nakedness to the Nakedness of Ultimate Being. It is natural in human marriage for couples to exchange gifts when they surrender themselves to each other. The same is true of spiritual marriage. We and God exchange words of love over and over until finally we cease to speak as separate beings. That-Which-Is gives Itself away as That which we are, speaks the Word that It is and we are, without intermediary, endlessly, without interruption. And just as the Godhead gives Itself away, we also give ourselves away, and that Self we give to It is again Itself.

> Having [God] for its own, [the human spirit] can give him and communicate him to whomever it wishes. Thus it gives him to its Beloved, who is the very God who gave himself to it. By this donation, it repays God for all it owes him, since it willingly gives as much as it receives from him.

> Because the soul in this gift to God offers him the Holy Spirit with voluntary surrender, as something of its own, ... a reciprocal love is thus actually formed between God and the soul ... in which the goods of both (the divine essence that each possesses freely by reason of the voluntary surrender between them) are possessed by both together. ... This is the soul's deep satisfaction and happiness: To see that it gives God more than it is worth in itself, the very divine light and divine heat that are given to it.[49]

---

[48] Jan van Ruysbroeck, *Op. Cit.,* 3.3
[49] John of the Cross, *The Living Flame of Love,* 3.78-80

In trying to define further this connection between the Godhead and us, John of the Cross said that *having been made one with God, the soul is somehow God through participation. Although it is not God as perfectly as it will be in the next life, it is like the shadow of God.*

Having returned to our divine roots, we *shadows* participate primarily in God's ongoing acts of *creation* and *compassion*. Perhaps people are so intrigued by the work of the author, painter, sculptor, composer, architect, or anyone who can fashion beauty from a blank slate, because of the affinity of their efforts to the Father's own creative, eternally birthing activity. Culinary artistry or fine needlework or even a home brewery can bring out the *genius* in us, in the original sense of that word, when they emanate from our highest Self. Those of us engaged in such work also acknowledge the need (can we say *compulsion?*) to keep working at our creations and to extend them out to others. We have no choice in the matter; it is a personal (and perhaps existential) imperative for every Creator.

> It is beauty that magnetizes the contemplative, and it is the duty of the contemplative to give beauty away so that the rest of the world may, in the midst of squalor, ugliness and pain, remember that beauty is possible.
> —Sister Joan Chittister

Participation in God's *compassion* is the culmination of our arrival at the top of Mystic Mountain, the ultimate creation that we give away to others and to ourselves. When we take part in the life of God, we discover God's Love deep within others and we do what we can to further their realization of that Love. Of such compassion, I will have more to say in the second part of this chapter, where I describe our return down the mountain and our heightened commitment to God's service.

The Transformed Body and Personality

We have said repeatedly that union takes place in the inmost recesses of the spirit where no thought or image can enter, in a previously unfathomable profundity unknown until now. Teresa of Avila wrote that we perceive the Godhead *in the extreme interior, in some place very deep within [us], the nature of which [the spirit] doesn't know how to explain.*[50] But Love also cloaks us like a protective sheath, and as we grow it expands to incorporate all creation, and we realize that it is no longer we who exist, that God alone fills all of creation with his Being. This God within, God without, condition is what Paul described when he wrote, *I live now, not I, but Christ lives in me* and further, *In him we live and move and have our being.*

Meister Eckhart stated this even more emphatically. He said of the Christ's nativity, *It would mean little to me that the "Word was made flesh" for man in Christ, granting that the latter is distinct from me, unless he also was made flesh in me personally, so that I too would become the Son of God.*[51] We are heirs of God not only in our *inner* being, but our very flesh and its impulses take part in the transformation. Body, mind, soul and spirit are finally aligned as they were in our original state of being. This is the household finally at rest. Thomas Merton wrote that *the fulfillment of our destiny is not merely to be lost in God ... but [to be] found in God in all our individual and personal reality*. And so it is with our beloved and precious fellow earthlings (or should we be calling ourselves *Godlings*?).

We may be reassured to find that our personalities and our individuality likewise are not lost, but rather attain to full realization in the state of Union. This is vividly clear when we read the stories of those who have reached transcendence. They are as different as Richard Rolle and Ananda Moyi Ma, as Madame Guyon and Gautama Buddha, as Rûmî and Lao Tzu. Augustine wrote: *When I shall cleave to thee with all my being ... my life shall be a real life, being wholly full of thee.*[52] When asked how monks deal with the changes that take place within themselves, Thomas Merton pointed out that a monk does not "change." Rather, he simply discovers who he really is.

In union we fully awaken to our true Self, to simple Awareness, and this Self views Its often chaotic universe

---

[50] Teresa of Avila, *The Interior Castle*, 7.1.7
[51] E. Benz et al (editors), *Meister Eckhart: Die Lateinischen Werke*, Vol. III, p. 101
[52] Augustine, *Confessions*, 10.28

patiently, without judgment, with God's own compassion. This is the divinization, or deification, of us mortal heirs of the divine, the only possible outcome of our merger with divinity, which leavens all with Its own Being. We are limitless because there are no limits to That-Which-Is (That-Which-We-Are). Our hearts have expanded to divine proportions. We have become, in the words of Sogyal Rinpoche, *the sky-like nature of our mind ... so natural that it can never be complicated, corrupted, or stained ... It is merely the immaculate looking at itself.*[53]

Our demeanor, interestingly, becomes extraordinarily ordinary, expressing the simplicity, the lack of complication we noted earlier. Simplicity and sublimity have merged, along with inner and outer serenity, buoyancy, gentleness and affection. This is to be expected once our small egos no longer have to prove their worth and our spirits are continuously reposed in God. We live humbly in this way, because we have seen the other side of ourselves and know we have no cause to trumpet our transformation. We are somewhat in the position of counselors in an alcohol rehabilitation center who can empathize with their patients/clients because they have undergone and recovered from the same addiction.

Historically, some who have scaled the summit have gone on to achieve great feats, but our approach to common endeavors more resembles the "little way" of a Therese of Lisieux. The portrait of the enraptured Buddhist monk leaning on his broom comes to mind, although rapture and ecstasy (and dryness as well) play little part in this new life. There are no public displays of oneness with God. Union is a given, accepted now as the normal condition of existence. So we are ordinary, although we know too that the divine spark at any instant, if it needs us, can burst our simple existence into flames and set our hearts ablaze.

> What, then, do I think makes someone a true man of the spirit? The most human people I have met have been the most spiritual, and vice-versa. I'm sure you've met at least one: someone who is tuned into every individual dial on the

---

[53] Sogyal Rinpoche, *The Tibetan Book of Living and Dying*, (San Francisco: HarperSanFrancisco, 1992), p. 49

human radio and pays attention to every piece of personal news as if it were a front page story; who makes you feel as if you matter without exalting you ... one who in no way imposes his or her beliefs on anyone but by example reveals what it means to be perfectly human; as someone who uses his or her free will to be compassionate to all.[54]

I believe it was G. K. Chesterton who said *people should know you're a Christian by the way you climb a tree.* In a similar vein, the wandering Rabbi Leib was asked what he'd learned of the Torah on his pilgrimage to Mezritch, the home of the renowned preacher Dov Baer. The Rabbi replied. "I did not go to the *maggid* to hear Torah from him, but to see how he unlaces his felt shoes and laces them up again."

And what shall we say of the joy that permeates this union? Probably it is best reflected in the early American hymn, "How Can I Keep from Singing?" Having recovered our uncluttered beginner's mind, we are prone to act like childlike fools of God, troubadours like Francis of Assisi or Jacopone da Todi—*at play in the fields of the Lord* as Peter Matthiessen put it. We come across this blissed-out figure over and over in the eastern stories of sages who try to communicate what they have seen, only to find themselves mocked as the village idiot. We share the delight of the Godhead as It gazes upon Its ongoing creation, the merry dance of the cosmos in which we are now participants, dipping in rhythm to the music of the spheres.

> An adult is one who has lost the grace, the freshness, the innocence of the child, who is no longer capable of feeling pure joy, who makes everything complicated, who spreads suffering everywhere, who is afraid of being happy and who, because it is easier to bear, has gone back to sleep. The wise man is a happy child.
> —Arnaud Desjardins

Immersed in the joyful Being of God, seeing the infinite at the heart of every event or scene, renews the spirit of youthfulness within us. As Isaiah wrote, *those who hope in*

---

[54] Richard John Friedlander, *Op. Cit.*, p. 108

Yahweh renew their strength; they put out wings like eagles. They run and do not grow weary, walk and never trip (40:30-31). Jewish spirituality goes so far as to say that joy is wisdom and preparation for prophecy, the very heart of religious living, the greatest of virtues.

Meister Eckhart preached that *people can never feel joy or pleasure in any creature if God's likeness is not within it.* Perhaps this is why he also warned his parishioners to mistrust those so-called "holy souls" who take no joy in creatures and whose spirituality is not centered in laughter. We hear of God's own joy repeatedly in his sermons: *With the same enjoyment with which God enjoys himself, he enjoys all creatures, not as creatures, but he enjoys the creatures as God. ... It is because of his great joy in giving that God wants a soul to be enlarged.* Elsewhere he added: *God has sheer delight and laughter over a good deed.* Evelyn Underhill wrote of the God-filled (or God-crazed) spirit,

> He may say something of the secret that the more decorous ... religion and philosophy will never let him—something, too, which in its very childishness, its freedom from the taint of solemnity and self-importance, expresses the quality of that inward life, that perpetual youth, which the "secret child" of the Transcendent Order enjoys.[55]

Laughter seems the healthiest response to life's absurdities and incongruities. The playwright John Gay thought so, and had inscribed on his tombstone,

> *Life is a game and all things show it.*
> *I thought so once and now I know it.*

Can it be that simple? From the perspective of eternity, yes, although it may seem more arduous on the time-space continuum when you consider the hard work and sacrifice involved. And yes, it can be that organic, a natural evolution through all the levels of human development into Oneness, for such is the course the Beloved intended for us from the beginning.

---

[55] Evelyn Underhill, *Mysticism*, 12th Edition, (New York: E. P. Dutton, 1961), p. 439

Through our transformation on ascending levels of human existence we come to understand at last what it means to be "in the world, but not of it." We feel rather like citizens of heaven, heavenly, more divine than human. This is life in God. We move on a loftier plane of awareness, a stratum indefinable using ordinary speech (although some of us can't resist trying). We can no longer be measured by the world's standards, nor does the concept of "standards" any longer make sense. Such delineation, categorization, distinction belongs to the world of dualism that we have long since abandoned. We see the whole of creation through the Godhead, the *one seeing* that Meister Eckhart noted, rather than seeing It through Its numerous manifestations. The latter may coalesce for us into a monogenetic bouillabaisse. We see That-Which-Is as It is in Its totality; creation forms but a small part of that vision.

Henry Suso, a disciple of Meister Eckhart, paints a striking portrait of day-to-day life in the world of the contemplative who has slipped within the Godhead:

> His being remains, but in another *form*, in another *glory*, and in another *power*. ... What then is this other form, if it be not the Divine Nature and the Divine Being [into which] they pour themselves, and which pours Itself into them, and becomes one thing with them? And what is that other glory, if it be not to be illuminated and made shining in the Inaccessible Light? What is that other power, if it be not that by means of his union with the Divine Personality, there is given to man a divine strength and a divine power, that he may accomplish all which pertains to his blessedness and omit all which is contrary thereto?[56]

I hate to dash even a droplet of cold water on this happy vision, but the pilgrim must wonder whether he or she has finally transcended human frailty in this union of Love. Unfortunately not. We don't reside in blissful union every instant once we reach the summit of Mystic Mountain; we still have to return to our home in the everyday world. We will constantly be reminded that human nature still clings to us

---

[56] Henry Suso, *The Little Book of Truth*, (New York: Paulist Press, 1989), Chapter 4

through our reactivity, people or events that still push our buttons, through the frustration of days that don't go smoothly, and a hundred events that bring us "back to earth." Even in union there are no guarantees of unbroken happiness. Perfect bliss is reserved for the final breakthrough alone, at our death. And while the ways in which we still come up short on this earth might be considered peccadilloes, they pain us as if they were major lapses. So long as we are still in our physical forms, and until our final breaths, we remain subject to the usual vicissitudes of life. Those who feel most secure in their exaltation are probably at the greatest risk. To paraphrase Rabbi Menahem Mendl, *those who think they are finished* are *finished*. Begging for divine mercy can never be overdone.

What we do realize most fully is that during trials, God moves with us, to be with and lay a healing touch on the hurting place within us, until the last trace of suffering finally melds into Love. We become caregivers to ourselves, recognizing at last that the vulnerable places within us are precisely the areas where God can best mend us. And we *will* be asked to interact with our external world, in many cases more so than before we attained to union, becoming caregivers to others. In these encounters our focus will be on service and helping to fulfill God's' plan than on personal excellence. We must continue the unending return to the brokenness within us and within others, as we guide these streams of suffering into the ocean of Love where they finally merge and disappear.

The Convergence of the Twain

It's significant that Meister Eckhart, in trying to describe the state of union, speaks of *one knowing* and *one loving* (in addition to the *one seeing* just mentioned). All along the pilgrimage route we have spoken of separate paths to the summit, of seekers who are drawn to the negative way of unknowing and nothingness, seeking union through the infinite, infused wisdom of the Godhead—and the positive way of those who seek the personal God and communion with the Beloved. On the path of emptiness, all human faculties are stripped to nakedness; the search for the Beloved, on the other hand, gradually fills the heart with divine Love. The ultimate, subjective experience of the first seeker is his or her absorption into the void; for the second, it is spiritual (or mystical) marriage between the spirit and the Beloved, an approach to union that traces back to the Orphic mysteries.

Among the Christian mystics, no two personify these attitudes more than Meister Eckhart, who seemed at times more Buddhist than Christian, and Teresa of Avila. He prayed, *God rid me of god*, from every image or thought man has ever had of "god." He wished to experience nothing outside the Godhead behind all images. Teresa on the other hand, as she entered the final two dwellings of her *Interior Castle*, felt even closer to the humanity of the Christ and to the Trinity, of which she said she had gained an understanding inconceivable to the intellect. Contemplating the mysteries of Jesus's life, she wrote, *dwelling on them with a simple gaze ... will not impede the most sublime prayer*. On the contrary, she added, an effort to forget Jesus and to live in continual absorption in the Divinity will result in a failure to enter the last two dwellings.

Teresa was not only the loyal daughter of the Roman Catholic church, she also had to be constantly vigilant against the Inquisition sniffing about her writings. Meister Eckhart, on the other hand, wished to be free of all human teachings. He also was a trained theologian and would have realized how the doctrine of the Trinity, for example, evolved over the first four centuries of church history to combat various "heresies"—very much a product of the human mind. He preferred to focus on the Oneness of Divinity rather than its myriad manifestations. That-Which-Is remains when all else disappears.

These two approaches to the Godhead are often referred to in spiritual literature as the *path of knowing* and the *path of being*. At the summit of Mystic Mountain, they come together in a single experience of Love as that Being integrates all within It and every separation disappears. At the summit we experience final reconciliation within ourselves as every aspect of our being unifies around the Self.

> Where there is duality, one smells another, one sees another, one hears another, one speaks to another, one perceives another, one knows another, but when everything has become the Self, by what and whom should one smell and see and hear and speak to and perceive and

know another? By what should one know that by which all this is known? How should one know the knower?
—*Brihadaranyaka Upanishad* 2:4:13

Because dualism no longer exists within us, for example, the prayer *forgive us our trespasses as we forgive those who trespass against us* is moot, because we recognize no trespass against us. *The losses we have suffered, the delight and peace we have experienced, the beauty we have known, all belong together in a profound way*, wrote John O'Donohue. All of our experiences, past and present, meld. The heart is content, having transcended the petty squabbles and differences that may have affected it in the past (and they are all petty from the higher perspective of union).

Our mind is the mind of God; our will is God's will; our memory is the eternal memory of God. In this state, intellect and will are reunited in divine Light and Love. It is Love, after all, that infuses sacred wisdom into our spirits. In terms of divine action, the two have never been separate. As the prophet Jeremiah said, *He sent fire into my bones and instructed me* (Lamentations, 1:13). This fusion of love and understanding is captured rapturously by Jan van Ruysbroeck in language suggestive of Teresa,

> When the inward and God-seeing man has thus attained to his Eternal Image, and in this clearness, through the Son, has entered into the bosom of the Father: then he is enlightened by divine truth, and he receives anew, every moment, the Eternal Birth, and he goes forth according to the way of the light, in a divine contemplation. ...
>
> To this all creatures must eternally be silent; for the incomprehensible wonder of this Love, eternally transcends the understanding of all creatures. But where this wonder is understood and tasted, there the spirit dwells above itself, and is one with the Spirit of God; and tastes and sees without measure, even as God, the riches which are the spirit itself in the unity of the living ground.[57]

---

[57] Jan van Ruysbroeck, *The Adornment of Spiritual Marriage*, 3.4

In another work, sounding more like Meister Eckhart, Van Ruysbroeck wrote,

> Such enlightened men are, with a free spirit, lifted up above reason into a bare and imageless vision ... and with an imageless and bare understanding, they pass through all works, and all exercises, and all things, until they reach the summit of their spirits. There, their bare *understanding* is drenched through by the Eternal Brightness, even as air is drenched through by sunshine. And the bare, uplifted *will* is transformed and drenched through by abysmal Love, even as iron is by fire. And the bare, uplifted *memory* feels itself enwrapped and established in an abysmal Absence of Image.[58]

In this second quotation, the personal aspect of That-Which-Is is hardly visible, yet all those abilities we value in our human personalities—action, understanding, will, memory—continue to operate, but are purified and raised to transcendent levels. *Eternal Birthing* and *abysmal Absence of Image* come together and both leave us awed and silent before the incomprehensible wonder of divine Love.

The breakthrough into divine Love at the pinnacle of Mystic Mountain is also a breakthrough into compassionate Love, a state in which empathy with our fellow beings and benevolent action trump contemplation. If we have not learned unconditional love before now, from parents or friends or our own generosity, we have the definitive model of such love in That-Which-Is. Given the fact of our free will plus our genetic and environmental conditioning, the Godhead unceasingly pours out Its Love on us with no expectation of reciprocation. If we *do* return that Love, it is, as John the Apostle wrote, *because he first loved us* (1 John 4:19) and continues to love us without reservation. God *always* makes the first move! As I mentioned earlier, when we recognize our lovability in the heart of the Godhead, when we can *love ourselves for God's sake*, we will have realized what Bernard of Clairvaux called the *highest degree of Love*.

---

[58] Jan Van Ruysbroeck, *Samuel* or *The Book of Truth*, Chapter 11.

It is this degree of Love, freely given and requiring no payback, which allows us to participate in God's compassion, to carry out the second part of the "greatest commandment," to love the dear neighbor as we love ourselves. In union, in the state of selflessness—understanding how the holy and the human are entwined—an unlimited capacity for compassion, God's own compassion towards others as well as towards us, arises within us.

Ultimately, we have no choice but to descend from the mountaintop, arms spread wide in a universal embrace, to do our part to further the divine plan for humanity and the cosmos at large. We no longer exist for our own sake, but rather to fulfill the divine will, to bring more abundant life to all of creation, into the entire time-space continuum, and we accept this task gladly because the divine will and our will are now the same.

> The voice of compassion is not absorbed with itself. It is not a voice intent on its own satisfaction or affirmation; rather it is a voice imbued with understanding, forgiveness and healing. ... Ultimately it is the voice of the soul.
> —John O'Donohue

After Enlightenment: The Return

> To go up alone into the mountain and come back as an ambassador to the world has ever been the method of humanity's best friends. ... The spirit of man, having at last come to full consciousness of reality, completes the circle of Being and returns to fertilize those levels of existence from which it sprang.
> —Evelyn Underhill

Staying forever undisturbed atop the mountain would be delightful, but our work is not done. Once *ox* is found in the Japanese ox-herding parable, the seeker returns to the crowded villages of the flatlands, often in the guise of a holy and bedraggled fool.

When Jesus was transfigured on the mountain, those who witnessed the staggering event wished to remain there and build altars to Moses, Elijah and their master, to "freeze" the other-dimensional in time and space. Instead he led them back down the mountain to resume their ministry. He also ordered them to tell no one what they had seen, as though they could somehow describe the indescribable.

The hero's journey and the pilgrim's way always end in homecoming. Home is clarity shed on our past actions and beliefs, a transparency that reveals to us what once lay obscured in the shadows of ignorance. With the wisdom and experience gained from pilgrimage comes understanding of what formerly perplexed us. As T. S. Eliot summarized in the final lines of his *Four Quartets*, we arrive with renewed vision at the place where we started and see it for the first time. Where we once saw a dull light in a leaden sky as we stood at the ocean's edge, we now see the full moon materialized from behind the clouds, skimming a brilliant moonbeam across the foam to our very feet. Welcome home!

We are like the nobleman in the gospel story (Luke 19:12) who journeys to a far country, is made a king and then returns home. When we set out on this pilgrimage, we had no inkling of the spirit's nobility or of our origin in Being, of the deification/reification that awaited us, but now we can accept divine inheritance as our birthright, albeit with humility, for we know we did nothing to earn it. In a commentary on this parable, Meister Eckhart pointed out that nobility and aristocracy have nothing to do with society's norms, but rather with a preference for the inner life over the superficial. *The person hidden within us is the inner person. Scripture calls this a new person, a heavenly person, a young person, a friend and a royal person. This person is meant when our Lord says that "a man of royal birth went to a distant country to be appointed king and afterward he returned."*[59]

What happens after union, then, after we have fully realized our spiritual nobility and make the trek back down the mountain? We share God's compassion and that compassion vents as action. We become conduits of grace and aid for others, agents of progress for the entire universe. We realize, in the

---

[59] Meister Eckhart, treatise *Vom edlen Menschen* ("Concerning the Aristocrat")

words of the *Course in Miracles*, "I am the light of the world. This is my only function. That is why I am here."

> Every morning, our first thought should be a wish to devote the day to the good of all living beings.
> —Dilgo Khyentse Rinpoche

In our frenetic, modern world we need mystics among us. The cities, the ghettos, have become the new desert, that place where the true worth of contemplatives is always tested. And it is from the reservoir of contemplative stillness and from hearts overflowing with God's own compassion that we as contemplatives can offer support and the opportunity for wholeness to those in need. Whole people, like the Roman Janus, simultaneously have an eye upon God and upon their fellow humans.

Loving the dear neighbor

> Souls brought to this state by the Lord ... look only at serving and pleasing the Lord. ... One of the greatest consolations a person can have on earth must be to see other souls helped through his own efforts. ... The more [such souls] advance in [contemplation], and the gifts of our lord, the more attention they pay to the needs of their neighbor.[60]

Bear one another's burdens, and so fulfill the law of the Christ, Paul wrote to the Galatians (6.2). As we rejoin our fellow beings, *service* takes on an entirely different hue from the palette of service described earlier in this book. We want our remaining years to make a difference in the universe. Service may continue to manifest as good works, depending on the needs of each individual we're helping, but these are only the outward signs of the change that has taken place in us. We now participate according to our measure in that divine-human life that mediates between man and That-Which-Is. And that *measure* is the extent of our awareness of God's call to each

---

[60] Teresa of Avila, *Meditations on the Song of Songs*, 7:8

person, which is also the extent of our personal connection to them.

> If you do not realize that the persons to whom you are relating are each called to an eternal relationship that transcends everything else, how can you relate intimately to [others] at [their] center, from your center?
> —Dom John Eudes Bamberger

This is what Anthony the desert father called putting our own souls in the place of the neighbors' souls, becoming a *double man* who suffers, weeps and mourns with them. And finally, he adds, it is as if we put on the actual bodies of our neighbors, suffering for them as we would for ourselves.

The rationale for loving the dear neighbor works like this. Because That-Which-Is has from eternity loved us first, we now can fully accept that we are lovable. We also have come to understand that this Being sees *all others* as uniquely precious too and we, as participants in Its infinite compassion, acknowledge their lovability as well. We love them because God loves them; we love them for God's sake, which is to say we love them, as we love ourselves, *in* the Godhead. Our rationale for loving, of course, is explained by and resides in the mind, but we discover in union that Love has also taken root in our hearts and triggers an outpouring from us to the rest of God's creation.

Love only grows, however, when we give it away; it can't be banked. Love that exists only in our heads is like a savings account that earns no interest while all the time losing ground to inflation. Love functions more like a muscle. The only way to strengthen and develop it is to exercise it.

Knowing that we share equally in God's gift of Love, our main desire is to awaken others' awareness of this compassion percolating within them. We see *Godlings* everywhere, particularly among our fellow humans who Thomas Merton called *people shining like the sun*. To our delight, we discover that the divine light refracted through the prisms we have become often ignites a spark of recognition in those with whom we come in contact. Wayne Teasdale speaks of *spiritual friendship* that responds to everyone we meet on that level:

> It requires a commitment to the spiritual development of your friends, the active work for their happiness and salvation, an essential and comprehensive understanding of another's inner state—really knowing our friends' hearts. ... It serves our friends' ultimate well-being.[61]

At the same time we recognize that not everyone is ready or wants to be awakened. People go about their lives at many different levels of consciousness, and for most the need is for basic survival or sympathy or other more fundamental type of help, which is simply where they are on their personal journey. Wayne Teasdale, who lived as a monk not inside his monastery, but on the streets of Chicago, addressed this form of love also:

> Why do I choose to be a monk in the world and not locked away in a remote hermitage? Because I want to identify with and be identified with all those who suffer alone in the world, who are abandoned, homeless, unwanted, unknown and unloved. I want to know the insecurity and vulnerability they experience, to forge a solidarity with them. The homeless are often open to the divine mystery through their very vulnerability and anxiety.[62]

The character of this Love we extend to the world, whatever form it takes, is best summarized in the oft-quoted passage in Paul's first letter to the fledgling Christian community in Corinth (1 Corinthians, 13:4-8):

> Love is always patient and kind; love is never jealous; love is not boastful or conceited, it is never rude and never seeks its own advantage, it does not take offence or store up grievances. Love does not rejoice at wrongdoing, but finds its joy in the truth. It is always ready to make allowances, to trust, to hope and to endure whatever comes. Love never ends.

Reminiscent of Paul's portrait is Henri Nouwen's description of the attentive and personal love he felt from the

---

[61] Wayne Teasdale, *A Monk in the World*, (Novato: New World Library, 2002), p. 81
[62] *Ibid*, p. xxix

Trappist monks among whom he lived for seven months in 1974:

> [These gentle men] show me love, show love to me not as an abstraction, but as a real individual with his own strengths and weaknesses, habits and customs, pleasant and unpleasant sides. The love they show me is very alert, awake, and based on the real me. When I ask something, they listen with attention and try to help me, and when I show a need for support, information, or interest, they offer me as well as they can what I need. So although their love for me is not exclusive, particular, or unique, it is certainly not general, abstract, impersonal, or just an act of obedience to the rule.[63]

We will need such unconditional, nonjudgmental patience and kindness as Paul and Henri described because we return to a world where God resides not only in peaceful stillness, but also where the sordid and violent reign, in senseless wars between nations and neighbors, in minds adrift on walkabouts, in the *barrio* and the basilica, the tenement and the temple.

> God is in every person's life. ... Even if the life of a person has been a disaster, even if it is destroyed by vices, drugs or anything else—God is in this person's life. You can, you must try to seek God in every human life. Although the life of a person is a land full of thorns and weeds, there is always a space in which the good seed can grow.
> —Pope Francis

Victims and perpetrators alike need our love. God's Being embraces within It all of earth's pain and suffering. If there is any validity to the notion of some Jewish authors that the *Shekhinah* suffers with us and among us, that our sorrow is God's sorrow, it only follows that through us the divine pain is eased and Its compassion bears fruit.

> The lowest of the low you can think of is dearer to me than your only son is to you.
> —Baal Shem Tov

---

[63] Henri J. M. Nouwen, *The Genesee Diary*, (Garden City, Doubleday & Company, 1976), p. 66.

Love is impartial, does not draw boundaries or limits, and is totally genuine. Nor does Love seek the pleasing or easy. *Easy*, as Dorothy Day might put it, would be if everyone walked about with *alter Christus*, (another Christ) stamped on their foreheads, but this is not the actuality of our planet. *Easy* is sitting in an overstuffed chair in an ivory tower, intellectually bemoaning injustice in the world or the plight of the poor with like-minded friends while doing nothing to alleviate that suffering.

Love accomplishes its purpose even in the midst of disorder, although it often moves so quietly and gently it goes unnoticed. In our muddled world where a huge segment of the population struggles just to endure while others buzz over the latest post to go "viral" in the social media, the real wonder of Love at work among us is easily ignored. It reveals itself within the normal movement of life's routines, not on some ethereal or supernal plane, not in lofty philosophizing, but in the cities and neighborhoods and the countryside where beleaguered survival is happening. As the two travelers to Emmaus discovered, the Christ does not reveal Itself in a glorified body, nor in a dazzling clarification of the scriptures, but in the simple act of breaking and blessing bread.

Love does not bend to what in the large picture are trivial biases or to personal preference or convenience. This is impossible for the enlightened spirit, for authentic Love springs from complete commitment of our true Self to the divine plan and to the Godhead's wish to evolve this plan through the breadth and height and depth of creation.

The evolving cosmic plan

> Just like space and the great elements such as earth, may I always support the life of all the boundless creatures. And until they pass away from pain, may I also be the source of life for all the realms of varied beings that reach unto the ends of space.
> —Śāntideva

In this compassionate condition, we wish more than ever to become the tools of Love, to put our limbs and minds and every aspect of our beings wholly at divine disposal, to help the entire cosmos move in the direction of enlightenment, of ever-rising consciousness. In the evolution of our species we have shifted from a geocentric view of the universe that placed us at the center of everything, to the heliocentric view of the Renaissance that placed the sun at the heart of our planetary system, to what we might now call a theocentric perspective— God's center everywhere. In our continuing evolution, we are moving towards a concept of Christ-Cosmic-Buddha-Consciousness expanding throughout the universe (or many universes) in which we are physically an infinitesimal part, but spiritually significant.

> All worlds are in need of exaltation and everyone is charged to lift what is low, to unite what lies apart and to advance what is left behind. ... And man is called upon to bring about the climax slowly but decisively.
> —Abraham Joshua Heschel

As Love transforms each of us as individuals, It also moves that many steps closer to transforming the entire cosmos.

When we speak of the universe evolving to the point of Cosmic Consciousness, or of the Cosmic Christ, we are describing the state of divine correspondence that the Creator envisioned from before time—and within time ever since It exploded into Love-become-observable at the Big Bang. Richard Rohr, in his work *Soul Centering through Nature*, described this divine consciousness as *God's plan to materialize his formless Spirit ... in visible form*, and added, *this mystery is going to* [be] *recapitulated at every level of creation as it evolves* [until] *in the end God will bring together everything under the title of Christ*. Our universe is a work in progress, ever in the process of unfolding towards completion, governed by laws such as gravity and entropy, and we now know by elements of chaos and chance and spontaneity, grinding its way through space and deep time. To us humans, caught up in the second-by-second progression of this slow dance (now 13+ billion years and counting), evolution towards Christ-consciousness seems agonizingly slow. From the standpoint of eternity, the expansion and contraction of the universe may be no more than an exhalation and inhalation of That-Which-Is.

> Creation is always in the heave of growth and becoming and when a thing journeys towards its own perfection or fullness of life, it is also secretly journeying towards the divine likeness.
>
> —John O'Donohue

We as a community and as individuals have been asked to participate in the continuing movement of the cosmos towards its highest potential. The choices we make will determine how such advancement happens. Those who chant or recite the psalms, for example, know that many of these songs call on all creation to join them in praising God. Protecting earth's natural resources would be an obvious way to participate—mending, repairing, and nurturing our continuously evolving planet. Our daily prayer is for God's Grace to allow each aspect of creation and each human individual at whatever level he or she currently lives, to advance one step closer to fulfillment, which is another way we serve as conduits of Grace.

We can no longer look upon ourselves solely as pilgrims passing through a single lifetime to work on our personal transformation, but rather, we must partake in making the universe whole, moving it forward. We are, fundamentally speaking, both elements in, and the summation of, an indivisible, inseparable totality of being.

> We are midwives in the between-times. The creation that is the cosmos, and each of us who feel lost on its threshold of becoming, need the midwife's powerful intent to pull us through. We need the midwife who lives in each of our souls to coach the birthing of an ever-new and renewing [human self]. We need to be midwife to others, lending our energy to their heroic attempts to break through barriers of the lifeless into new life. Together we need to midwife the world.[64]

Contemplation vs. action

Since the days of Martha and Mary, the traditional Biblical representatives of the active and contemplative paths to

---

[64] Christin Lore Weber, *Blessings*, (New York: HarperCollins, 1989), p. 34

spirituality, the debate has simmered over which chose the "better part." Jesus, of course, gave the nod to Mary, for which the contemplative orders have been ever grateful. Always nice to have your lifestyle approved by the (Son of) Man. On the flip side, a student told Shunryu Suzuki about an experience in which he dissolved into amazing spaciousness. "Yes, you could call that enlightenment," the Roshi opined, "but it's best to forget about it. How's your work coming?"

Jan van Ruysbroeck summed up the state of union as one of *absolute repose, absolute fecundity*, suggesting a balance between contemplative composure and service, or rather that while active in the world, we remain in God, centered in the stillness at the core of our being. Although we have withdrawn from the world at times during our practice, we no longer shun it, but instead enter into and pray from the center of all this humanity. Our quiet inner space becomes a place where others can meet God, like that favorite house in the neighborhood in which we grew up where all the kids were welcome to hang out, those who were lonely in their own homes most of all. We remain immovable in God, while simultaneously alive to the suffering inherent in the human condition. *Now the Spirit of God says in the secret outpouring of our spirit: Go ye out, in an eternal contemplation and fruition, according to the way of God.* This is when the spirit imitates the eternal birthing of the Godhead, delivering its offspring, its mystical children, into the world in the form of kindheartedness, generosity and renewed spiritual vitality.

> And this is why the interior man lives his life according to these two ways; that is to say, in rest and in work. ...Because the soul is just, it desires to pay at every instant that which God demands of it. ... He dwells in God, and yet he goes out towards all creatures in a spirit of love towards all things ... *And this is the supreme summit of the inner life.*[65]

Love has usurped every aspect of our being and now acts through us. We are like musical instruments through which the divine orchestration blesses the world, the flutes through

---

[65] Jan van Ruysbroeck, *The Adornment of Spiritual Marriage*, 1.2.45

which the Its breath creates the most tender and heartening melodies. Should we ever harmonize as one, we could become a "flash mob" symphony of compassion.

Teresa of Avila viewed Martha and Mary as coequals and coworkers inspiring the innermost dwellers in her *Interior Castle*. Of the shift from delight in contemplation to service to one's neighbor, she wrote,

> The soul is asking to perform great works in the service of our Lord and of its neighbor. For this purpose it is happy to lose that delight and satisfaction. ... A person's life will become more active than contemplative. ... Martha and Mary never fail to walk almost together when the soul is in this state. ...
>
> Much good is done by those who, after speaking with His Majesty for many years when receiving his gifts and delights, want to serve in laborious ways even though these delights and consolations are thereby hindered.[66]

Meister Eckhart, predictably, had a unique take on the Martha-Mary story. In his sermon on Luke 10:38 and Jesus' visit to the two women, he imagined Martha as the older, more spiritually advanced of the pair, and Mary, basking in the master's words, as the neophyte, still learning and taking pleasure from spiritual delights. Only later would she be fit for the highest service. As Catherine of Genoa experienced, *[spiritual pleasures] are more difficult to eradicate once we become attached to them. Not to understand this is to be barred from the one perfect good—God pure and naked*. Perhaps, Meister Eckhart suggested, this was one of the concerns that prompted Martha to ask that Mary get up and help with the meal.

Be that as it may, Martha worked *among things, among cares*, but these things and concerns did not own her. Like a good existentialist, she worked from the depths of her being, detached from the outcome of her labor. She was centered in the *one thing necessary*, the *one perfect good*, namely *God pure and naked*. She lived in the world, but was not of it, as is true

---

[66] Teresa of Avila, *Meditations on the Song of Songs*, 7.3, 7.7

of anyone in this highest state of Union. If we work outward from within the Godhead, from within eternal Love, everything we do honors that Being. If we don't pray formally or sit in contemplation, it is because we have *become* prayer and our every action emits prayer. This is why Augustine could exclaim, *love and do what you will*!

Meister Eckhart no doubt would have maintained that insofar as we have not integrated our activities and our contemplative side, we still dwell in dualism. We still see a distinction and a separation within Love. In the spiritually mature mystic, there is no partition between action and introspection. They are one state of being. Service to others does not compete with contemplation. Rather it deepens our spirituality and our connection to the Godhead. Love is compassion made visible, and compassionate action is of one nature with contemplation. The greatest saints were prodigious field workers.

Living in depth like Martha, we go the extra mile to help others. We don't cater to weariness. We find, on the contrary, that in the midst of our activity, divine energy infuses us with a surge of dynamism. We discover also that because we are no longer fearful, we can help others release their fears, the main source of dualistic barriers. We can dissolve in Love situations that used to be frustrating or threatening for us or for others. We can appreciate our dear neighbors, interact freely with them, love them selflessly, steer them gently towards their highest spiritual potential—or feed, clothe and house them if that is the more urgent task. Again, we meet each person on his or her level of present need.

We have become, in a sense, *bodhisattvas* who, out of compassion, vow to help all sentient beings eventually rise to Buddha consciousness, achieve enlightenment and freedom from *samsara* and its cycle of death, rebirth and suffering. I should add (for those who might be concerned about the rest of creation) that in Tibetan and Japanese Buddhism, the term *sentient beings* does include plants and inanimate objects. The bodhisattva mindset spurs each of us to act in ways that advance our universe towards fulfillment of the cosmic purpose.

The bodhisattva

Mahāyāna Buddhism is based principally upon the path of the bodhisattva, which can take one of three directions. The first of these is the path of the *king-like* bodhisattva who aspires first to achieve Buddha consciousness and then to return in a state of full realization to help the rest of creation attain the same enlightenment. Its advocates would insist that we cannot lead others to enlightenment until we are enlightened ourselves. Those Buddhists who prefer the other two paths would consider this the lowest way, however, because it seeks its own benefit first.

On the second path, the *boatman* bodhisattva is still working to achieve enlightenment. He ferries the rest of us across the river of *samsara* and simultaneously ferries himself across.

Finally, the *shepherd* bodhisattva deliberately postpones entry into the bliss of nirvana, choosing to remain in our world of illusion until all souls have been saved. These are the good herdsmen who make sure their sheep arrive safely ahead of them and place the welfare of all others ahead of their own. For this reason, some consider theirs the highest of the three paths. Avalokiteśvara and Śāntideva are believed to be examples of the shepherd.

In a sense, these three paths reflect the historical development from Hīnayāna Buddhism (which stressed personal liberation and internal growth) to Mahāyāna Buddhism (which emphasizes compassion for others). They also mirror the Christian and Zen mystical evolution from early self-absorption in the desert or the mountain cave to an awakened desire for selfless service in the world.

Besides the Buddhist bodhisattvas, there are any number of semi-legendary teachers and saviors believed to be at work in the world, such as the White Brotherhood of Angels and Ascended Masters and the eight Chinese Immortals revered by Taoists. Their mission is to raise our individual and collective consciousness, awakening us to the divinity within each of us. The *totally* legendary British contribution, of course, is Doctor Who, the time lord who out of compassion travels throughout time and space to save humans and nonhumans from all sorts of physical danger while imparting a bit of wisdom and understanding and even occasional sympathy for the alien "monsters."

Also worshiped by Taoists is Lao Tzu, the author of the *Tao te Ching*. He is often represented as the Tao personified, sharing his teaching with humanity for our salvation, and is considered by some to be a deity. Religious Taoists maintain that he has undergone numerous "transformations" throughout history, taking on various guises through numerous incarnations to initiate seekers in the Way.

While not specifically thought of as bodhisattvas, Judaism has its tradition of the Lamed Vav Tzaddikim, the thirty-six just men, so hidden that they themselves don't know who they are. They are usually poor, obscure, and unrecognized, peasants and porters, the ones who bear all the sorrows and sins of the world. Needless to say, this keeps the disciples of renowned holy men busy speculating whether their particular teacher could be one of the thirty-six, although their speculation can never be confirmed.

This group of righteous beings "greets the *Shekhinah*," the Divine Presence, and their virtue and faith alone convince God to preserve the universe, even when immorality defines mankind as a whole. As long as they continue to serve humanity and God, the cosmos will continue to exist, but should God at some point be unable to find someone just enough to replace a dying tzadik, creation will at once come to an end, a macro-version of Sodom and Gomorrah.

We can only imagine how difficult it must be for the bodhisattva to surrender supreme bliss to help the likes of us (although they're well aware of God's Love for us). In a letter to the Philippians (1:21-25), Paul voiced the agonizing deliberation all such saints likely go through when trying to decide whether or not to retrace their steps down the mountain. Having experienced transfiguration at the summit, the return to everyday existence would be excruciating except for their love and desire to manifest God's will during what is left of their time in human form.

Life to me, of course, is Christ, but then death would be a gain. On the other hand, if to be alive in the body gives me an opportunity for fruitful work, I do not know which I should choose. I am caught in this dilemma: I want to be gone and to be with Christ, and this is by far the stronger desire — and yet for your sake to stay alive in this body is a more urgent need.

Love is strong as death, but just how strong is death? For these saints there is the happy knowledge that in the end when the timing is right, that is, when God wills, the invitation from death will release them into unending bliss. For them, as for all contemplative souls, death has lost its sting.

Chapter 5. Death, the Ultimate Breakthrough

> Life is a luminous pause between two great mysteries, which themselves are one.
> —Carl Jung

So here we are at the end of the road, where our next step will plunge us into infinity. This will be the final and the biggest step we will ever take.

As contemplatives we likely will have no fear of death and, in fact, like Paul writing to the Philippians, we may welcome it. Death is, after all, the bridge the lover crosses to join the Beloved. We may be as blasé as the dying Therese of Lisieux in this conversation with one of her novices:

"Then death will come to fetch you?" the girl asked.

"No, not death," Therese replied, "but the good God. Death is not, as pictures tell us, a phantom or a horrid specter. ... It is the separation of soul and body—no more! Well, I do not fear a separation that will unite me forever to God."

Eterne and Return

The crossing from this life to the next completes our life circle. We return to the point where we began, to that eternal realm we left when we entered time. We entered our bodily forms at birth and will set them aside at death. Viewed from the other side, our spirits *left* the timeless zone when we took on human life and will *return* there at our death.

As the quotation from Carl Jung suggests, the between time on this earth is *luminous*. As we have learned on our journey, divine light sometimes radiates from our centers at those moments when time brushes up against eternity. Although we assume the form of flesh and blood, our human entity, because it is grounded in the essence of the Godhead, remains one with that essence throughout our earthly existence.

I believe that the One Great Mystery is revealed at the beginning and forever beckons us forward toward its full realization. Most of us cannot let go of this implanted promise.

—Richard Rohr

In his "Ode. Intimations of Immortality," poet William Wordsworth wrote that *our birth is but a sleep and a forgetting*—not entirely a forgetting, however, for *trailing clouds of glory do we came from God, who is our home.* In our early years we are unaware of this link for the most part. Living in ignorance, we fail to view creation with God's vision, as an eternal now, a single seeing without distinctions of past and future. We forget where we came from and seldom wonder about our existence outside time. We may be trailing clouds of glory, but the clouds soon dissipate as we launch into our earthling lives. Could we but retain our original awareness, we might be tempted to sing out with Eternal Wisdom,

> Yahweh created me when his purpose first unfolded,
> before the oldest of his works.
> From everlasting I was set firm,
> from the beginning, before the earth came to be.
> The deep was not when I was born;
> no springs gushed with water.
> Before the mountains were settled,
> before the hills, I came to birth.
>
> —Proverbs 8:22-25

Despite the initial forgetting induced by the touch of angel Leila, however, there remains the mystery that constantly beckons and leads us to speculate about existence before time and after time. Once we understand that we enter life and will leave through the same portal, the arc leading from and back to that gateway takes on deeper significance. Our life journey becomes a pilgrimage.

The Ascent through awareness and love

Looking back on that pilgrimage, we can view the climb to the summit of Mystic Mountain as an ascent through *increasingly rarified levels of awareness*. We are led up that path through a series of breakthroughs, with every step like an escalator subsuming the one below it.

We begin with the most obtuse form of consciousness, our breakthrough into creation and the inarticulate awareness of infancy. From there we grow into the ego awareness formed in the external world. Once we became aware of Love's invitation, however, we feel summoned inward by a wish for *something more*. This embryonic consciousness of the divine slowly awakens to God's omnipresence, the face of God shining through visible creation (including through *us*). This is still a "dense" earth-based revelation, though far more subtle than our early, unaware view of the universe. The world is still natural, but no longer illusory. Following many years of preparation, of self-cleansing and self-discipline, we are next stunned by the awareness of God dwelling within us and more amazingly still, of us dwelling within God. Following that encounter, if we are so favored, we experience the influx of the Spirit of Love, are eased from *becoming* into *being*, resulting ultimately in blissful union with the Godhead that dwells behind and beyond the created universe.

Looked at from another angle, the path up Mystic Mountain is also an ascent through degrees of Love. John of the Cross well understood that *Love alone is what guides and moves [the spirit], and makes her soar to God in an unknown way along the road of solitude*. Our entire journey, then, is illumined by Love, beginning with the love we feel from our father and mother. Because that early love sets the pattern for our love of others, we can hope it is unconditional, not contingent on how much we do or don't inconvenience our parents.

On the mystic way we experience various expressions of love directed towards the infinite. In *The Dark Night*, for example, John described the progression from feelings of fervor in our earliest practices (*The Dark Night*, 1.1.2), to worries about serving God well enough during spells of dryness (1.11.2), followed by a longing for God on the sense level, although this is not yet "fire" (1.11.1), feelings of *esteeming* love mixed with fear of losing God or the sensation of God's absence in the depths of darkness (2.13.5) and finally of a passive, impassioned enkindling of Love in the spirit (2.11.1-5; 2.13..3-

9). We love "authentically" at this level, *with all our heart, all our soul and all our strength* (Deuteronomy 6:5).

This last is not yet the height of love, however, for our spirits are still stumbling in darkness during these stages. John used the term *mystical marriage* for the first time in his *Spiritual Canticle* to describe the inseparability of God and us in union, in which our spirits merge and disappear forever into the boundless ocean of Love.

> When there is union of love, the image of the Beloved is so sketched in the will, and drawn so intimately and vividly, that it is true to say that the Beloved lives in the lover and the lover in the Beloved. Love produces such likeness in this transformation of lovers that one can say each is the other and both are one. The reason is that in the union and transformation of Love, each gives possession of self to the other and each leaves and exchanges self for the other. Thus each one lives in the other and is the other, and both are one in the transformation of Love.[67]

This is the breakthrough into the shared, compassionate divine Love that spills over into our love for others. John called this but a *sketch* because, once again, we still wander the earth in our temporal shells and still must deal with the limitations of human existence. He went on to say that the portrait will be perfected only after our final breakthrough into "glory."

> [Transformation in this life] cannot be perfect and complete even though the soul reaches such transformation of Love as is found in the spiritual marriage, the highest state attainable in this life. Everything can be called a sketch of Love in comparison with that perfect image, the transformation in glory. [68]

Strangers in a strange land

When Moses fled Egypt, he lived for a time in Midian where Zipporah, his wife, gave birth to a son (Exodus, 2:22). He named the boy Gershom, which has been variously interpreted

---

[67] John of the Cross, *The Spiritual Canticle*, 12.7
[68] *Ibid.*, 12.8

as "a sojourner there" or "I am an alien in a foreign country" or "stranger in a strange land."

As exiles from eternity, we can share his sense of banishment. We are all sojourners here, never fully at home. Historians tracking the story of humanity create the impression that we evolved to colonize the planet, given the way we've spread over its surface, but in fact we have been set down in a good-sized schoolyard. We've been handed a period of time that we can waste staring out the window of our classroom, busily texting notes to one another, or goofing off in general—or we can use it gainfully to watch and learn and prepare ourselves for the passage back to our homeland.

Our sense of dislocation can be even more intense if we are born into a spiritually-impoverished culture enamored with "stuff" and "more stuff." Children in some parts of the world, such as many Asian countries, drink in spiritual insight and the notion of deity with their mother's milk. In our Western culture, studying or practicing integral wisdom is rarely part of our upbringing, which can lead to many detours and misdirections along the way. Consequently, we have to try harder and pray harder for divine assistance to prepare us for death and beyond, hopeful that God's mercy will make allowance for our handicaps. No matter what our background, however, we have to go through many practice "deaths," ultimately dying to everything transient, before we can set foot on the threshold of never-ending Love.

The flow of our years in time might be compared to the passage of a river through a series of unpredictable landscapes. Water evaporates from the great sea and descends on earth as rainfall at the headwaters of an infant rivulet. As it builds from there, it drifts or ripples or rages through the decades of our lives, vanishing in the end back into the ocean of its beginning. The river's movement does not pass unnoticed, however. Throughout its course limitless Love overshadows its movement, even when it overruns its banks and floods out of control. Even then, at its most destructive, its main thrust is still downstream, headed always towards final fulfillment in the embrace of that timeless sea.

If we are well prepared by the time we receive death's invitation, we feel ready to wave goodbye to those still waiting on the shore, and empty ourselves into the brightness of the boundless deep. Jewish wisdom calls this *devekut*, "melting into the divine."

> All the great rivers, that is to say, the Ganges, the Jumnâ, the Aceravati, the Sarabhu, the Mahî—these, on reaching the great ocean lose their former names and identities and are reckoned simply as the great ocean.
> —Vinaya-Pitaka

Approaching Death

> I am making my last effort to return to that which is divine in me, to that which is divine in the universe. ... I am striving to give back the divine in myself to the divine in the All.
> —Plotinus

The contemplative practices described in this book are trial runs preparing us to dance with death. We have made death our companion quite deliberately and look forward to its tender embrace, that last waltz to the strains of "Good Night, Sweetheart." The many changes we experienced along the way—our withdrawal from the external world, sinking inward, nondualistic thinking, overcoming the sense of a separate self, discovering the deep silence at our center, touching the sacred and merging at the end with Divinity—are all rediscovered in an accelerated form as we approach death. Time winds down and the entire admixture of life distills to a final ... heartbeat.

> It is well for a man to depart to the forest ere the four bearers carry him away amidst the laments of his folk. Free from commerce and hindrance, possessing naught but his body, he has no grief at the hour of death, for already he has died to the world.
> —Śāntideva

When we die, we disappear into that Love from which we materialized at birth, as though being drawn through a wormhole into another dimension, the dimension of sheer *Isness*. We lay down our bodies and enter eternal life as pure spirit. The infinite no-place on the other side has no further need of our human senses or intellects or willpower. We experience at last the final breakthrough past the veil that separates time and eternity.

In earlier years, I wrote grant applications on a freelance basis for nonprofit agencies, knowing that as soon as I was successful and they had secured their funding, they would have no further need of my services. So it is with our once-useful bodies and minds and the strenuous efforts of our wills that worked so hard, with the aid of grace, to transform us. They've achieved their end and put themselves out of work. This is where we chortle in our joy: *Oh frabjous day! Callooh! Callay*!

Fear of Dying

Death ideally should be the triumphant culmination of a life well-lived. Nevertheless, none of us knows for certain how we will die, under what circumstances, or what the mindset will be in that last instant despite our many years of "practicing" death in contemplation. We may die surrounded by the affection of family and friends; we may die suddenly and alone in a traffic accident or violently on a battlefield. As one comedian put it somewhat darkly, *I want to die peacefully in my sleep like my grandfather, not screaming and yelling like the other people in his car.*

We can hope that somewhere inside us we are conscious of our dying and that we can surrender to it with serenity. Releasing to death in joyful equanimity is the key to final tranquility, and the sooner in our lives we do this, the more peaceful will be our end. And once again, surrender means active participation in the process, the act of dying in this case, entering as fully as we are able and with as much awareness as we can muster into our final moments.

Kathleen Dowling Synge wrote that mere *acceptance* of one's plight is *dying while living*, while *surrender is living while dying*. Describing a woman in the final days of life with whom she interacted as a hospice worker, she wrote: *As she entered surrender, the overwhelming verbal motif was gratitude—gratitude for her family of origin, for her husband and her daughter, for the good fortune life had brought her, for her plants, for the movement of wind on the water, for the arrangement of petals on a rose, for that last sip of tea.*[69]

For many of our fearful fellow beings, however, the unreserved letting go that death asks of us means the loss of all we thought we were, all we achieved or accumulated, which in turn spawns the commonplace terror of death or resistance to it. Poet Dylan Thomas urged his father not to go gently into the darkness, but rather to rage against it. Imagine the loneliness one may feel at that moment as everything slips away. We might be totally terrified at the prospect of our finite selves going extinct, sinking forever into oblivion. *If we must leave, at least not now,* we protest, trying perhaps to bargain with God. We want more time to see unborn grandchildren, to finish incomplete projects like the dying writer in Ernest Hemingway's "Snows of Kilimanjaro," to attend future weddings and graduations, to make sure our children are grown and well on their own, able to fend for themselves, to know and be remembered by our grandchildren, to tell friends and family all those things we meant to say, but didn't, *et cetera*. But the real question is: *will we ever have enough time to make our lives and the lives of all those nearest to our hearts turn out the way we'd like?* We'd do better to work on that one long before old age!

Until death every ending in our life has marked a beginning. As the saying goes, when one door closes, another opens. We come to believe our story is *never*-ending because we always continue in our physical forms on to the next adventure. We carry on, living as many different people in the span of a lifetime. This is not true in the case of death, however. Death unravels the entire warp and woof of our earthly weaving, cuts us from the loom—the body, knowledge, memories, ideas, feelings, relations, creations, joys and sorrows. All of them gone with the last exhalation. There is no continuity, no subsequent event, no subsequent breath. The timeline ends and we launch across the infinite distance that separates the final heartbeat of earthly life and the first experience of bodiless, mindless afterlife. We may scream our objections, in our heads at least,

---

[69] Kathleen Dowling Singh, *Op. Cit.*, p. 229

but the scream fades without no echo into the absolute silence we are entering.

This fear felt by those unprepared for death is why they so often need us beside them. Knowing what a dying person experiences can make our time beside the deathbed not only a valuable opportunity for service, but also a chance to learn and review our own preparedness. We can delay our private mourning at a loved one's passing rather than disrupt the stillness of the deathbed. This is a sacred space where the body and blood of the dying are being transformed into spirit in a reverse transubstantiation. While what we say is intended to soothe, listening is equally important. The words and even the silence of the dying carry a weight capable of touching the listener to the depths. The dying do not waste their few remaining moments on the trivial. They speak as little, utter as few syllables, as necessary. These are their last minutes on earth, and they have no more time for the insignificant.

In her wonderful summation of the waning days of physical life, Kathleen Dowling Singh described how, when all the striving and desiring no longer make sense, the dying are left with only the here and now, even those who have never practiced contemplation. When attachments become pointless and possessions mean nothing, only the true Self remains. This is the grace in terminal illness. We might compare these suddenly unburdened latecomers to the workers in the parable who arrived at the last hour and received the same pay as the men who had labored all day—a glorious paean to God's generosity. But what a blessing those among us also know who experience enlightenment before death!

> If transformation into the final stage of consciousness, the merging of individual, personal identity into its Source, has not occurred prior to the time of dying, the Nearing Death Experience suggests that dying, in and of itself, activates this potentiality. ... As we die, the Ground of Being discloses itself, drawing our consciousness back into it.[70]

---

[70] Kathleen Dowling Singh, *Op. Cit.*, p. 17, 220

Kathleen also compares the act of dying to *an awakening from the dream of form through the chaos of dissolution*. This slow process of dissolution leads the individual through phases of turmoil, surrender and finally transcendence. The inner life of the terminally ill comes together in a refinement akin to the purgation of the mystical journey. Sometimes this beautiful tuning manifests physically. The worn expression begins to convey a deepening radiance as Love suffuses the *blue-bleak embers* of the fading life and they *gash gold-vermillion*.

> At the moment of death, the soul experiences the same impressions and passes through the same processes as are experienced by those who are initiated into the Great Mysteries.
>
> —Plutarch

Those who seem most fearful and unready for death, however, still can sense at the heart of their being that death will not destroy them. Even if they have not made a friend of death beforehand, there is something about it that invites them to trust it to steer them beyond mortality to peace. Whatever it does to the body and the mind and the ego, it cannot alter the spirit. At some level the dying understand that the nothingness they have always believed they should fear will actually free them from the ego's endless cajolery and its lifelong attempts to prove and protect itself—usually to their detriment. At last they can get that *monkey-mind* off their backs.

Death's approach awakens us furthermore to how That-Which-Is has always given itself away in the minutia of our daily lives. This is the classic instant when life flashes before our eyes. We are finally aware of the full import, the larger picture of every detail that has accompanied us from the first day of our journey. When my wife's former husband died of cancer, his final words seemed to reflect this insight. After many years of theological quandary, he smiled, "It's obvious"—words that also sum up the completion of the contemplative way.

Why, I?

When we stand back and review this enigmatic circle of life, we confront questions that have plagued rational men and women forever—that is, those relying on reason alone. Why would an eternal Being, supremely content in Itself, need to split into three or into ten thousand? Why the creation? Why do we pass from mystery and back into mystery in these fragile human shells? Why could we not simply remain in Oneness, in the eternal Source of our being, in our original condition? Was our original condition an inferior sub-enlightenment that cannot be completed until all existence achieves Cosmic Consciousness? Is creation the original divine comedy? There is that story of the Atman scattering Itself into innumerable "pieces" that then must work their way back into the Atman through innumerable incarnations. That's entertainment on a pretty vast scale. In the *Brahma Sutra* we read, *Brahma's creative activity is not undertaken by way of any need on his part, but simply by way of sport in the common sense of the word*. Was Shakespeare right when he wrote in "King Lear," *as flies to wanton boys are we to the gods; they kill us for their sport*? Is all the world really but a stage?

> Man is made to be the plaything of God and this, truly considered, is the best of him. ... We ought to live sacrificing and singing and dancing, and then a man will be able to propitiate the Gods.
>
> —Plato

In primitive society it was enough that we were here (however we arrived here), surviving in a hostile environment and eking out a life by the sweat of our brows. We were born, procreated and died. The reason was beyond human understanding, although the god or gods who created and ruled everything knew why. Some among us have always been inquisitive, however, and have come up with a number of answers to the ultimate riddle.

John of the Cross believed the reason for our existence is to realize union with God. He saw this as *the most noble and sublime state attainable in this life*. Rûmî carried this notion a step further, bridging the ideas of the playful God and John's view of the human quest for union:

> You contrived this "I" and "we" that You might play the game of worship with Yourself, that every "I" and every

"thou" should become one soul and be submerged at last in the Beloved.

Going beyond personal realization, others have felt that the purpose of the entire cosmos is to realize Spirit, to give It form through creation, to *embody* Divinity. The *Guru Granth Sahib,* the sacred scripture of the Sikhs, commented that *simply to define God, millions await rebirth.* Meister Eckhart agreed: *God cannot know himself without me.*

> God ... so copied forth himself into the whole life and energy of man's soul, as that the lovely characters of Divinity may be most easily seen and read of all men within themselves. ... The *impress* of souls is ... nothing but God himself, who could not write his own name so as that it might be read, but only in rational natures.
> —John Smith (the Platonist)

The Godhead propels us into time and place to discover Itself in us and us in It, that It might be born in our spirits and our spirits into It, and that we might experience the kingdom of heaven even while we are in this world. Truly, this spiritual quest is the *game* of life, and why God requires us to play, who knows? Weren't we aware of our One Being before we assumed physical existence? Everything written in this book about existence before birth, as well as the Buddhist tradition, assumes a state of "original mind." Apart from all speculation, however, this *possibly necessary* trek across the terrestrial globe is the reality of our existence. If nothing else, it's a marvelous adventure. The quest for home literally gives meaning and purpose and enjoyment to our time on the planet.

> "From where do you come?" someone asked the holy Râbi'a.
> "From the other world."
> "And where are you going?"
> "To the other world"
> "What are you doing in this world?"
> "I am making a game of it."
> —'Aṭṭâr

Earlier, I quoted Bede Griffiths regarding the inpouring of Spirit:

> This was the very purpose of creation from the beginning, that body and soul, matter and mind, man and the universe, might be moved by the Spirit and drawn into the divine light and life.

Elsewhere he enlarged on that comment:

> The very purpose of creation was that the One should be able to communicate himself to the many, that finite and temporal beings should come to participate in the infinite and eternal being and consciousness of the One and experience the bliss—*Saccidananda*—of the Supreme. And this bliss is a bliss of love. Love seeks to communicate itself, and the purpose of love would not be satisfied if there were no one to share that love.[71]

In this view, the Godhead created us out of necessity. Before creation, Ultimate Being had no capacity to *express* love because It *is* love. Creation gave It this capacity, for now It had something and someone to love, an entire cosmos in which to manifest Its wisdom and joy and glory, which It does in a celestial symphony in which each manifestation is an instrument tuned to eternal harmony.

Life after Death

> No, I don't believe that I will be lost after death. Why should You have made me fruitful, if I must be emptied and left like the crushed sugarcanes? Why should You spill the light across my forehead and my heart every morning, if You will not come to pick me, as one picks the dark grapes that sweeten in the sun in the middle of autumn?
> —Gabriela Mistral

Presumably everyone who has read this book to these final pages believes, like the Chilean poet, that God will harvest and carry us into the afterlife. We believe not only that *our* spirits do not die, but also that every friend and relative who has preceded us in the final transition has not died once and

---

[71] Bede Griffiths, *The Marriage of East and West*, , (Springfield: Templegate Publishers, 1982), p. 98

forever. They have merely set aside their borrowed bodies and awakened to eternity, as we too will soon do.

Questions arise, however, when we speculate about the nature of this afterlife. What exactly does Oneness with Ultimate Being mean in terms of the spirit's condition? Does our education in spirituality continue after death? Do we remain on hold while we await reincarnation to resume our learning on earth? Every culture has its theories, from the Buddhist void to complete absorption in the divine to souls continuing into the next world with their "human" personalities intact, but we're still waiting for someone to return with a definitive answer. We really don't know what to expect after death.

In favor of total and final immersion in the Godhead, Henry Suso wrote in *The Book of Truth*,

> Mark this: in eternity, all creatures are God in God, and there no fundamental difference exists between them. ... And insomuch as they are in God, they are the same life, the same being, the same power. They are the same One, and nothing less.

Most of the Christian mystics quoted throughout this book would have agreed and even the Hindu Ramana Maharshi, sounding much like Suso, stated emphatically that *one cannot see God and yet retain individuality.*

The vibrant John O'Donohue objected strongly to this view, however:

> It seems unlikely that life would choose us so carefully, bring us through so much and then simply offload the whole harvest of journey over a cliff. ... So much could not have been so carefully built to be simply destroyed in a second. Something more profound and ultimate is happening behind the veil. ... Eternal life must mean that neither the person nor their world is lost. Eternal life must

mean the continuity beyond death of that individual life and that individual world.[72]

Given all we've said about the small self and the true Self, though, it would seem that most of what we've built over the years would fall into the category of excess baggage. Stephen Levine wrote that much of our fear of death stems from *the imagined loss of an imagined individuality*. Would we want to drag that "imagined world" into the afterlife with us? And can't this business of going *through so much* apply also to the life of a tree or a stream in its determined path to the sea? Do these aspects of our world also continue after our death?

Appeals to individual saints and our remembrance of deceased family members and friends, the sensation (or hope) that they somehow remain near us, suggest most of us want to believe in the extension of our human characteristics and relationships. John O'Donohue again:

> The dead are not distant or absent. They are alongside us. ... Because we cannot see them does not mean that they are not there. ... Though they cannot reappear, they continue to be near us and part of the healing of grief is the refinement of our hearts whereby we come to sense their loving nearness.

We seek the help of saints, although mostly in terms of "church-assigned" functions, rather than their former personalities. "Saint Anthony, help me find my car keys." "Dear Saint Anne, bring me a man." Bury a statue of St. Joseph upside down in the yard to sell a house. In my own profession I should invoke the help of Francis de Sales, the Roman Catholic equivalent of the Muse. While such prayers can seem frivolous or superstitious, invoking the departed historically has led to many supersensory events and healings that we consider miraculous, or otherwise inexplicable, lending credence to this popular view of "heaven."

---

[72] John O'Donohue, *Beauty* (New York: HarperCollins, 2004), pp. 205, 211

Heaven is not a place, of course. It is a state we can experience even in this life, the *kingdom among us*, as near to us as the Godhead Itself (and what is nearer?). It would follow, then, that all the spirits held within the heart of that Love would be accessible to us also. We can experience this celestial state even if we cannot see it. Similarly, we can contact the unseen spiritual beings residing within it through the many forms of verbal and mental prayer, meditation and contemplation. Some have even made themselves "visible," resuming their former human appearance, to those seeking their advice or help.

In *The Pharsalia*, Lucan said of the Druids, *from you we learn that ... death is the center, not the finish, of a long life.* The implication of his comment is that our education may not end with this lifetime, but may continue after death in some form of spiritual university, and perhaps through many more incarnations on earth. It may be that further breakthroughs await us as we continue the journey in nonphysical form. Presumably, for those who have attained union with the Godhead, further training will not be necessary and the cycle of rebirth will be broken, which in Hindu terms is the supreme goal of humanity.

Still speculating, I can imagine that we might experience the "heaven" we expect. The Muslim experience will be different than the agnostic or Jewish or Christian experience. So while we may meet the Buddha on the road in the course of our earthly pilgrimage, we won't meet him in the afterlife because he'll be off in some void of nothingness.

And what exactly is *eternity*? Is it a string of endless days, months, years? We might assume there is no timeline after death and no sense of place, although the purgatory tale suggests there may be a location where purgation is measured in time, and where alms from a friend may buy us an indulgence and release us from some of that measurable interval. Is there a post-death state where our "dross" is once and for all "burned away," whether or not it happens in a *place* still bound by *time*? Does purgation in fact continue after death for those who haven't arrived at union with That-Which-Is? Or do we carry our baggage, our karma, into another lifetime? Is there a spiritual forum where our education continues after life, or between lives?

This author can't allege any special revelation—from God or through his messengers—of the sort popular in the 1930s or claimed by the founders of religious sects over the centuries. I'm as curious as the next person as to what we will see when we finally meet the Godhead *face-to-face*. Even Paul, who said he was rapt up into the third heaven, still admitted that he saw *as through a glass darkly*, just like the rest of us.

Commenting on the *Ten degrees of Love according to Bernard*, John of the Cross writes of the final degrees,

> I will mention no more here than that this step of the ladder of love [the ninth] is succeeded by the tenth and final step, which is no longer of this life. The tenth and last step of this secret ladder of love assimilates the soul to God completely because of the clear vision of God that a person possesses at once on reaching it. ... John says, *we know that we shall be like him* (1 John 3:2), not because the soul will have as much capacity as God ... but because all it is will become like God.[73]

Most of us, I'm sure, can live with this prospect. For now, we only glimpse the eternal Light through occasional and brief flutterings of the veil, but this final transfiguration of our spirits and the refinement of our vision as the veil at last drops will be death's magnanimous gift to each us.

Among those convinced that reincarnation is inevitable as we continue our education, we also come across the concept of "pods" of spirits interlinked for eternity who help each other advance by assuming different roles during their series of lifetimes. *This round we can switch and I'll be your husband and you the wife, so you can better understand the feminine side of divinity.* Those who espouse this theory base their case on a number of hypnotic sessions in which those hypnotized were questioned about their memories of the time between-lives.

---

[73] John of the Cross, *The Dark Night*, 2.20.5

This possibility doesn't particularly surprise me. When I met my wife, my first words were, "Oh, there you are," as if to say, "I haven't seen you in centuries." I suspect our reactions will be similar when the veil falls away and we finally encounter the Godhead "face-to-face," something along the lines of "Oh, here I AM."

$$\Omega$$

Suggested Reading

An Interrupted Life: the Diaries of Etty Hillesum 1941-43, Washington Square Books, 1985.

Anonymous, *The Cloud of Unknowing and The Book of Privy Counsel.*

Arrien, Angeles, *The Four-Fold Way*, HarperSanFrancisco, 1992.

Bernard of Clairvaux: Selected Works, Evans, G. R., translator, Paulist Press, 1987.

Buber, Martin, *Tales of the Hasidim*, Schocken Books, 1947.

Campbell, Joseph, *The Hero With a Thousand Faces*, New World Library, 3rd Edition, 2008.

Catherine of Genoa, *Purgation and Purgatory, The Spiritual Dialogue*, Hughes, Serge, translator, Paulist Press, 1979.

Davies, Oliver, editor, *The Rhineland Mystics: Writings of Meister Eckhart, Johannes Tauler, and Jan Van Ruusbroec and Selections from the Theologia Germanica and the Book (Spiritual Classics),* Crossroad Publishing Company, 1990.

Douglas-Klotz, Neil, translator, *Prayers of the Cosmos: Meditations on the Aramaic Words of Jesus*, HarperCollins, 1994.

Doyle, Leonard J., translator, *St. Benedict's Rule for Monasteries*, Liturgical Press, 1948.

Föllmi, Danielle and Olivier, *Offerings*, Stewart, Tabori & Chang, 2003.

Fox, Mathew, *Breakthrough: Meister Eckhart's Creation Spirituality*, Image Books, 1980.

French, R. M., translator, *The Way of a Pilgrim*, Harper, 1954.

Friedlander, Richard John, *Paradise Besieged*, Flying High Press, 2009.

Griffiths, Bede, *The Marriage of East and West*, Templegate Publishers, 1982.

Heschel, Abraham Joshua, *A Passion for Truth*, Jewish Lights Publishing, 1973.

Julian of Norwich, *Revelation of Love*, Skinner, John, translator, Doubleday (Image Books), 1997.

Kavanaugh, Kieran & Rodriguez, Otilio, translators, *The Collected Works of St. John of the Cross*, ICS Publications, 1991.

———————, *The Collected Works of St. Teresa of Avila* (3 volumes), ICS Publications, 1987.

Kisly, Lorraine, editor, *Ordinary Graces: Christian Teachings on the Interior Life*, Bell Tower, 2000.

Law, William, *A Serious Call to a Devout and Holy Life*, Printed for Wm. Innys, 1929.

Matthiessen, Peter, *The Snow Leopard*, Bantam Books, 1981.

Matt, Daniel C., *The Essential Kabbalah*, HarperCollins, 1995.

Nouwen, Henri J. M., *The Genesee Diary*, Doubleday & Company, 1976.

O'Donohue, John, *Beauty*, HarperCollins, 2004.

Rohr, Richard, *Falling Upward*, Jossey-Bass, 2011.

———————, *Immortal Diamond*, Jossey-Bass, 2012.

Ryan, Regina Sara, *Igniting the Inner Life,* Hohm Press, 2010.

Sack, John, *Yearning for the Father: The Lord's Prayer and the Mystic Journey*, Hohm Press, 2006

Singh, Katherine Dowling, *The Grace in Dying*, HarperCollins, 1998.

Sogyal Rinpoche, *The Tibetan Book of Living and Dying*, HarperSanFrancisco, 1992.

Suso, Henry, *The Little Book of Truth*, Paulist Press, 1989.

Suzuki, Shunryu, *Zen Mind, Beginner's Mind,* Shambhala Publications, 1970

Swami Prabhavananda & Isherwood, Christopher, translators, *How to Know God: the Yoga Aphorisms of Patanjali*, New American Library, 1953.

Teasdale, Wayne, *A Monk in the World*, New World Library, 2003.

Tutu, Desmond, *An African Prayer Book*, Doubleday, 1995.

Underhill Evelyn, *Mysticism*, E. P. Dutton.

Ward, Benedicta, translator, *The Sayings of the Desert Fathers,* Cistercian Publications, 1984.

Weber, Christin Lore, *Blessings*, HarperCollins, 1989.

Wilbur, Ken, *A Theory of Everything*, Shambhala Publications, 2000.

Wu Ch'êng-ên, *Monkey,* Waley, Arthur, translator, Grove Press, 1943.

About the Author

John R. Sack was born in Springfield, Ohio. He has a BA in English from Yale University and an MA in Creative Writing from the University of Washington.

As a young man, he entered Our Lady of Gethsemane Trappist Abbey in Kentucky where Thomas Merton was his novice master. Years later, he trained in a Hindu ashram in Ganeshpuri, India. Spiritual awakening and transformation are common themes in both his fiction and nonfiction books.

Other works include the internationally-acclaimed novel, *The Franciscan Conspiracy* (currently out in 16 languages) and a companion work, *Angel's Passage* (available in three languages). *The Wolf in Winter* is a fictional tale of the early career of Francis of Assisi. Other fiction and short stories can be seen on his Amazon or Smashwords author pages. His nonfiction *Yearning for the Father* is a guide to contemplative prayer based on the Lord's Prayer.

Today, he is happily writing and homesteading at Casa Chiara Hermitage, situated on a sunny mountainside in southern Oregon, with his wife, Christin Lore Weber, author of many books related to spiritual growth. They have three grown children and one grandchild in their blended family.

Feel free to contact John at cyberscribe2@hotmail.com.

Made in the USA
San Bernardino, CA
18 February 2014